RULE 1 OF INVESTING

RULE 1
OF INVESTING

HOW TO ALWAYS BE ON THE
RIGHT SIDE OF THE MARKET

MIKE TURNER

REGNERY
PUBLISHING
A Division of Salem Media Group

Regnery® is a registered trademark of Salem Communications Holding Corporation

Cataloging-in-Publication data on file with the Library of Congress

ISBN 978-1-62157-874-1
e-book ISBN 978-1-62157-875-8

Published in the United States by
Regnery Publishing
A Division of Salem Media Group
300 New Jersey Ave NW
Washington, DC 20001
www.Regnery.com

Manufactured in the United States of America

10 9 8 7 6 5 4 3 2 1

Books are available in quantity for promotional or premium use. For information on discounts and terms, please visit our website: www.Regnery.com.

*I dedicate this book to my wife, Sue, who is
and always will be the love of my life!*

Contents

INTRODUCTION

THREE QUESTIONS TO ASK YOUR ADVISOR

The three most important questions you can ask yourself (if you are your own money manager), or your professional money manager:

1. "Do you plan to change how you manage my money in bull markets as opposed to bear markets? If so, please explain:
    a. "Exactly what is your bear market strategy in comparison to your bull market strategy"
    b. "Exactly how will you know (please be specific) when the market has moved from a bull market to a bear market?"
2. "If you do not plan to change how you manage my money in a bear market, tell me how much will I lose before you move me to cash?"
3. "Do you ever go to 100% cash? If not, why not?"

If you manage your own money, or want to, you must come to terms with the above questions. If you have someone managing your investment capital, please ask them to answer the above questions and insist that they answer them specifically. And make sure you get answers to your exact questions. Most professional money managers will give you reasons why they are good managers without actually and directly answering these questions.

You do not want to hear answers like:

"Depending on the market, we change our allocation strategies to take advantage of lower risk opportunities that fit the best use of capital at the time." This is just financial gobbledygook and obfuscation. Make them tell you exactly how they grow AND protect your capital.

Or...

"In bear markets, we move more toward defensive investments that have a strong track record of outperforming in bear markets." This is just another way of saying, "We are perfectly content for you to lose money in a bear market, so long as we can show you that you lost less than the market."

Think about it this way...If the market drops 50%, as it did in 2008, and your portfolio drops 40%, your money manager could brag about how, due to his/her investment acumen, you beat the market by 20%. Never mind the fact that you actually lost 40%!

With regard to Question 3 above, when you talk to your money manager or review the mutual funds you like to follow, do you ever wonder why they almost never simply go to cash? I'm going to show you in Chapter 1 how going to cash at the right time can almost double your return, but financial investment firms (for the most part) never go to cash. There are two reasons for this:

1. If they go to cash, they think you will say, "Why should I pay you to manage my money when all you are doing is sitting on cash. I can sit on cash myself and not have to pay a management fee," or,
2. If they go to cash, back-end bonuses and commissions are either not paid or are lost. You see, most financial firms make the most money from you by keeping your money in

the market and getting kick-backs (commissions) from the investments they put you in. These commissions and kick-backs are not required to be disclosed to you and, what's worse, they create a huge conflict of interest between doing what's best for you and what's best for your manager's total income. You need to be very careful doing business with any investment firm that avoids moving you to cash in high-risk markets.

THE TRUTH ABOUT BUY-AND-HOLD:

You have been told that buy-and-hold is smart investing and that trying to time the market is a fool's game. In reality, both are terrible investment strategies.

The entire financial industry, as well as major financial figures like John Bogle, Jeremy Siegel and Warren Buffet, a host of mutual funds and even watch-dog organizations like FINRA and the SEC promote, either directly or indirectly, the merits of a "long-term investment strategy" with a buy-and-hold mindset. So...what exactly does this term "buy-and-hold" mean?

Investopedia defines buy-and-hold as follows: *Buy-and-hold is a passive investment strategy in which an investor buys stocks and holds them for a long period of time, regardless of fluctuations in the market. An investor who employs a buy-and-hold strategy actively selects stocks, but, once in a position, is not concerned with short-term price movements and technical indicators.*

There are several reasons why this strategy is promoted — some of them reasonable and some not so much. A legitimate argument for buy-and-hold is if you buy the stock of a high-quality company and that company prospers in a growing economy. The odds of the stock's share price will also grow, and in some cases, substantially increase.

Unfortunately, this does not represent the entire aspect of what can occur to your investment capital when you use a buy-and-hold investment strategy.

When buy-and-hold is promoted as a smart strategy, there are three assumptions made that are never explained to the investor:

First Assumption: You will never need the money (otherwise, you fail the "hold" part).

Second Assumption: You will live forever (that way, you can wait as long as needed for the market to "come back").

Third Assumption: You don't care if your investments drop by 50%, 60% or even 90%. The reason you are told not to worry about losing money in the near term is because "the market always comes back."

Investors are rarely aware of the fact that once a large amount of capital has been lost, it can take decades to just get back to even. Many investors do not consider that if they lose 50% in a major market decline, their investment basis will have to grow by 100% just to get back to even.

The bulk of the private investment advisory world wants you to have a "long-term investment horizon." They perpetuate the myth, promulgated incessantly by a host of famous, very successful portfolio advisors and managers, that if you simply buy equities consistently over many years, you will be basically dollar-cost-averaging[1] your way into the market, and "if you are in the market for the long-haul" you will do far better than the high-risk, low-return 'market-timers.'[2] The proponents of buy-and-hold will extol putting money to work in the market, and simply sitting back and watching how that money can double, triple or grow even more in the intervening years. And, if you just go back far enough in time and wait long enough, these claims of massive returns are true. What these buy-and-hold proponents fail to include in their narrative is the huge losses that occur when bear markets are encountered. These proponents

---

1 According to Investopedia: Dollar-cost-averaging is an investment technique of buying a fixed dollar amount of a particular investment on a regular schedule, regardless of the share price. The investor purchases more shares when prices are low and fewer shares when prices are high.

2 According to Investopedia: Market-timing is the act of moving in and out of the market, or switching between asset classes, based on using predictive methods such as technical indicators or economic data. Because it is extremely difficult to predict the future direction of the stock market, investors who try to time the market, especially mutual fund investors, tend to underperform investors who remain invested.

will gloss over the amount of time (sometimes decades of time) it takes to get back to even. They will counter the massive losses by saying, "if you continue to buy in a falling market, you will be buying more shares for the same dollars, and eventually those bargains will come back to reward you with huge gains." All true, if you live long enough and never need the money. But, there is a much better way, and a much less risky way, to invest in the market. Chapter 1 will describe this methodology in detail.

Privately, many of those professionals who promote buy-and-hold will say, "The average investor is not smart enough to know when to get in and out of the market. So, buy-and-hold is designed to provide a way for (in their words) investors without the proper ability to make the right decisions at the right time to grow their capital when investing in the stock market.

Mutual fund managers (and most of the large financial investment firms) want you to believe they are using the most advanced, highest-quality investment strategies to invest your money in the stock market; and, they want you to believe that buy-and-hold is how the smart money invests. They fool you into thinking they are so good and so smart by doing a little investment sleight-of-hand. Here is how they do it:

- "Window Dressing" where large funds and managed accounts report performance on a quarterly basis. In reality, they could and should report daily, but most do not. Just before the end of the quarter, these firms sell their worst performing stocks and buy the equites that have been outperforming for the past quarter. They do this so that you will assume they have been smart enough to hold only the best performing stocks in their funds and you will ignore the fact that the fund lost money in the past quarter or, at best, underperformed. If you believe in buy-and-hold, you will not question short-term losses and you will be fooled into thinking your money is being managed by really smart people who know how to pick the best stocks, even though they did not pick those stocks until the last

day or two of the quarter…just before reporting results
and holdings.

Most mutual funds want you to buy into the buy-and-hold concept,
because they are very afraid to hold cash. In fact, most write the inabil-
ity to hold cash into their bylaws, and use that as an excuse to remain
fully invested all the time—even in a bear market. Why? Because they
are afraid that if they go to cash, you will pull your money out of their
fund as you can hold cash yourself. These same companies will tell you,
"Only the weak hands and unsophisticated investors go in and out of
the market…chasing profits that they never find." They shame you into
not going to cash.

Lastly, the buy-and-hold promoters will point to the 'other side of
the coin': Active Management, which is also misidentified as "market-
timing". As much as they would like you to think the only two choices
are "passive investing" (buy-and-hold) or "market-timing," where the
objective is to guess when the market will top or bottom in the future,
these are NOT the only choices you have. They will trot out study after
study after study showing how much better passive investing is in the
long run over active investing (i.e. market-timing). They want you to
draw the incorrect conclusion that there are only two choices: buy-and-
hold or high-risk market-timing. They fail to mention the third major
investment strategy: Market-Directional Investing, which I discuss in
detail in Chapter 1.

ACTIVE VERSUS PASSIVE INVESTING (THE REAL TRUTH):

The financial industry wants to lump every failed or weak investment
strategy that is not buy-and-hold into one big bucket called "Active Investing" or "Active Management". They want to take the myriad of studies
(that they have run themselves or paid to have run) where they compare
the success of portfolios to buy-and-hold or passive investment strategies.
These studies almost universally support the notion that passive investing

outperforms active investing if the length of time is long enough, and if the study duration does not include a disproportionate amount of time devoted to a bear market.

In other words, these studies cherry-pick timeframes and types of markets to 'prove' passive buy-and-hold strategies outperform Active Management.

Despite these skewed, biased studies, there is no small amount of truth in the fact that trying to pick future market tops and bottoms is nothing more than a guessing game; educated guessing or not...it is still a guessing game.

So What Makes Market-Directional Investing So Different?

Market-Directional Investing is NOT based on guesswork, and it does NOT try to pick future market tops or bottoms. Market-Directional Investing relies on math, rules and discipline (more to come on this in Chapter 1).

No one knows what the future market or stock price is going to be. No one knows how long a current trend will last. Trying to guess the future is a fool's game and rarely is it successful; it is *never* successful in a long-term investment strategy.

So, any Active Management strategy that relies heavily on guesswork is bound to be wrong a lot. Like a stopped clock, a guesswork strategy will be right periodically, but it is far too risky to be betting your capital on an occasional correct guess.

In Chapter 1, you will learn exactly how to always be on the right side of the market. You will learn how to know when to be bullish, when to be bearish, and, perhaps most importantly, when to be in cash. In Chapters 2 through 10, you will learn to maximize your returns in bull and bear markets by knowing what to buy, what to sell, when to sell, when to short and when to cover.

Get ready to become a world-class portfolio manager. Welcome to the world of Market-Directional Investing!

PROLOGUE

My first book, "10: The Essential Rules for Beating the Market," provided readers with a solid foundation for learning how to become a world-class, rules-based, disciplined, non-emotional investor in the stock market. That book is as valuable today as when I wrote back in 2008. Indeed, much of that first book is encapsulated in this book, "Rule One for Investing". But, if you have already read my first book, please do not skip through the rules, thinking you already have them mastered. Many have been updated and improved *In many ways, those rules are as valid today as they were ten years ago, But there was something missing that I knew could help investors take their approach to a whole new level....* Let me tell you what I discovered, and how this book came about... A few years ago, I pulled together my R/D team and tasked them with a new project. I told them to look at every losing trade I had ever made in my lifetime and statistically determine why the trade lost money. [If you have ever bought and sold stocks in the stock market, you have learned that, regardless of your investment acumen, not every trade turns out to be a winning trade.]

My rules-based methodology keeps me from having a lot of losing trades, but I wanted to see what I could do to reduce that number even more.

I wanted to know if my team could determine what went wrong in each trade and if we could learn something that we could incorporate into our rules-based investment strategy that would reduce the number of losing trades and, by extension, increase the number of winning trades. Did we encounter a losing trade because we did not follow all of my rules? Was it because one or more of my rules did not work? Or…was it 'something' that my rules did not cover? I'll be honest with you; I had my suspicions and told the team to look at how the market was moving when we lost money in a trade.

After several days of intense analysis, my team came back with their results. In some cases, bad news would come out about a company (sometimes the management team, sometimes the products, sometimes the competition, etc.) and the stock's price would suddenly reverse and trigger a stop loss exit and, hence, a loss.

But we also found that many times, I would buy a stock that met *all* the rules for fundamental scoring, technical scoring, sector and industry scoring, and we still lost money. The problem:the market was rolling over or moving lower. Sure enough, soon after buying the stock, the drag of the market would have a significant impact on the stock's price and it would suddenly reverse trend, hit the stop and we'd exit with a loss.

Granted, none of the losses were significant because of our stop loss strategy (covered in detail in this book), but they were losses nonetheless.

This got me to thinking…My Technical Rule did not have a scoring component for the market. My first thought was to simply add another component to the Technical Rule and then back-test that to see if that would help reduce the number of losing trades.

THE EPIPHANY

One night, as I was lying in bed, thinking about how I was going to add "the market" to my Technical Rule; how many points I was going to assign to it; how I was going to measure it; etc...A thought came to me like a thunderbolt. What if I was looking at this all wrong...What if the role the market plays in making more winning trades was NOT just a component of technical analysis? What if "the market" is everything? To be specific, What if the technical direction of the market was more critical to capturing a winning trade *than any other analytical component*? **What if market direction was "Rule One"?**

I could hardly sleep the rest of that night and couldn't wait to put my team on this "Market Directional Epiphany".

The next morning, I called my team back together and gave them the following assignment: Go back through all of my trades (winners and losers) and ONLY consider trades that were made when the market (a composite of the S&P 500, S&P 400, NASDAQ, Dow-30 and the Russell 2000) was trending higher. After another few days, they came back to me and they all looked stunned. I couldn't wait to hear the results:

- The number of losing trades plummeted to only a handful.
- The winning trades far outnumbered the losing trades and generated far greater net returns.

The team lead said, "These results are so astoundingly good, why doesn't everyone use this methodology?"

More testing was done and more refinement was achieved. Here is what we concluded:

1. Don't even consider putting on a new trade unless the market is trending higher.
2. Don't try to guess when the current trend will end, but constantly measure the current market trend to mathematically know when the trend has ended. This meant that our trading was predicated on the fact that the current trend in the market will continue until it doesn't. So, we had to

come up with mathematical algorithms to determine, explicitly, how to measure that event.

3. Avoid major whipsaw events by following a moving average surrounded by a volatility band, such that when the market is above the band, we are permitted to buy long positions; when the market is inside the band, we look to raise cash by selling existing positions; and, when the market is below the band to look for short plays, including the use of inverse ETFs.

I cover the details of how this works in this book. The beauty of this methodology is it completely removes the need to guess about trends or how long they will last. You never have to try to time market tops or bottoms. You will always know when a market has topped and when it has bottomed and how to trade accordingly. And, above all else, this methodology forever puts the nail in the 'buy-and-hold' coffin. Using the rules and discipline that I lay out in this book will always keep you on the right side of the market. You will never fear getting caught in the next bear market and you will always be able to capitalize on bull markets.

This, my friend, is what I call "Market Directional Investing," It starts with making sure you are always on the right side of the market, or as I call it: "Rule One for Investing." It is revolutionary and above all else, it works.

I hope you enjoy the book and more than that, I hope you become wealthier because of it.

Mike Turner

CHAPTER 1

MARKET DIRECTIONAL INVESTING

"How to more than double your return by simply going to cash at the right time."

Never miss out of bull market opportunities and never fear bear markets again, for the rest of your life!

THE MARKET-DIRECTIONAL INVESTMENT METHODOLOGY CONCEPT:

I am fairly certain you have experienced the following at some point in your trading history: You do all the right research. You find a stock with great fundamentals. Technically, the stock is trending higher. The sector and industry are both trending higher. Everything about this stock makes it look like a sure thing (although you know there is no such thing in the world of stock market investing). You buy the stock and it initially does exactly what you thought it would do—trend higher in share price. Then, seemingly out of the blue, something happens in Washington, or the economy, or some geopolitical event unfolds...and the market, as a whole, begins moving lower. Initially, your sure thing stock holds up, but as the market continues to weaken, your stock suddenly begins to tank.

Transition Zone Definition: The center of this Zone is the 200-day moving average of the market, or a stock or an index or an ETF. The width of the Zone varies in width over time. It is predicated on the most recent 12 months of volatility of the entity being monitored. In Figure 1, the "entity" is the SPY. The top of the Zone is calculated by adding one standard deviation of normal volatility of the SPY (in this case) to the 200-day moving average. The bottom of the Zone is calculated by subtracting one standard deviation of normal volatility from the 200-day moving average. And just to be clear, this Zone is NOT a Bollinger band.

Before you know it, you're down in the position; initially only a little, but the damage continues to mount. You make the mistake of listening to the buy-and-hold crowd that promotes dollar-cost-averaging and you double-down on your losing trade. Finally, you've lost so much money that you can't stand the downtrend anymore and you sell out of your sure thing stock for a substantial loss.

You have experienced the frustration of buying the right stock for all the right reasons and at the right time, but the market moved against you and your stock enough to completely reverse the upward pricing trend you so expected to happen.

In the past, you probably wrote this off to the vagaries of the market. After all, no one can predict what the market is going to do in the future. You say to yourself, "Oh well, just bad luck, I guess." No it wasn't bad luck. What you failed to do was assess whether the market was supporting or not supporting your trade and even if the market was supporting your trade initially, you failed to get out of the trade when the market quit supporting it.

You ALWAYS want the market, as a whole, supporting your trade. No stock can continue, indefinitely, to move higher in price if the entire market is moving lower. In this chapter, I will show you how to

I find it interesting that Warren Buffett, in his 2017 letter to shareholders, advised that losses of 50% or more are not only possible but inevitable in the future. And just to keep this in perspective, below is a table of Berkshire-Hathaway historical losses. I will show you how to avoid these kinds of losses in your own portfolio.

Date Range of Losses	Amount Lost
March 1973 to January 1975	-59.1%
Oct. 2-27, 1987	-37.1%
June 1998 to March 2000	-48.9%
Sept. 2008 to March 2009	-50.7%

Data source: Berkshire Hathaway 2017 annual letter to shareholders.

dramatically improve your odds of buying the right stock at the right time, in the right market.

You need to know when to be a buyer, a seller or simply to go to cash. In other words, you need to know when to invoke a bullish or bearish investment bias, or when to get completely out of the market.

I will cover some critically important concepts that will put you on the path to long-term success in the market. When using my Market Directional Investment Methodology, you will actually look forward to bear markets. You will never be on the wrong side of the market. If the market is bullish, you'll have a bullish investment bias. If the market is neutral, you'll be going to cash. If the market is bearish, you'll have a bearish investment bias.

And, *guessing* what to do and *guessing* when to do it, will never again be a part of your investment strategy.

Let's get started by looking at the Three Immutable Laws of Investing:

FIRST LAW

THE CURRENT TREND WILL CONTINUE UNTIL IT DOESN'T

Please take a look at Figure 1, below:

There are 3 lines on the chart:

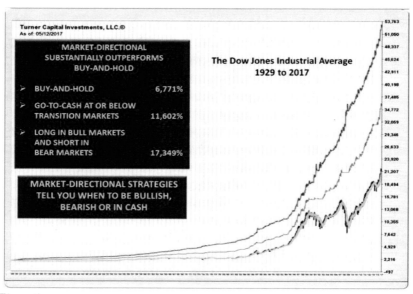

Figure 1

1. The <u>bottom line</u> is the Dow's weekly closing prices for roughly 88 years. If you had put $100 to work in the Dow in January of 1929 and held on to it for 88 years, that $100 would have grown nearly 8,000 percent.

2. If all you did was go to 100 percent cash <u>after</u> the DOW moved into the transition zone, you would have doubled your money to almost 16,000 percent <u>and</u> missed all the bear market crashes.

3. By shorting the DOW when below the transition zone, you would have made almost 20,000 percent...a far cry better than buy-and-hold.

You should notice that there are actually two lines, superimposed on each other, in the "bottom line" of the chart above. The black line represents the week-ending close of the Dow. The yellow line is the "Transition Zone" (see "Transition Zone Definition", right). It is the single most important component of this first law's methodology. For the scale of this chart and 88 years represented, you cannot discern the actions on-going inside this Zone on this chart, but I will give you much more readable examples as we move forward in this chapter, so don't worry about knowing all the details at this point.

4. The <u>middle line</u> represents the results that you can achieve by simply selling everything in your portfolio and go to cash when the market stops its bullish uptrend and exhibits a trend reversal (yes, I will show you how this is measured a bit later). Keep in mind this chart does not take into account any income from interest or dividends. So, 100% of the time, when the market stopped climbing higher, the model simply moved from being 100% invested to 100% cash. Notice that by going to cash at the right times, the total return for the 88 years almost doubles from 6,771% to 11,602%. How does going to cash almost double your return? Simple: Holding cash, which in this model makes nothing, is far better than losing money. Plus, if you don't lose a significant amount of capital in a bear market downturn, you've got money (that you didn't lose) ready to go back into the market when the market goes back into a bull trend. And…I know what you're thinking… "Just how did you know to go to cash, Mike, if you weren't guessing what the market was going to do in the immediate future?" That is a great question and it lies at the very heart of my approach to market-directional investing. Just keep reading…I will show you exactly how to know when to go to cash and NEVER guess about what the market is going to do in the future.

5. The <u>top line</u> on the chart, above, represents a growth of nearly 300% better than buy-and-hold. To get this kind of return:

- You are 100% long the market when the market is in a bullish trend.
- You are 100% cash when the market is in a transition zone (yellow line in Figure 1).
- You are 100% short the market when the market is in a bearish trend.

I assume, by now, you must be asking, "How do you know when to be bullish, in cash, or bearish?" That, my friend, is why this book is worth so much more than you paid for it. I will show you specifically how that determination is made a little further into this chapter.

SECOND LAW
MEASURING WHERE THE MARKET IS, MATTERS MORE THAN GUESSING WHERE IT MIGHT BE IN THE FUTURE

I want you to understand the meaning of the phrase, "trend analysis," as I use it. Trend analysis is both an exact and an inexact science. Certain parameters must be established before this term can be properly identified and used. There are two major components to defining a trend, in the world of market movements: time and price. Trends can be measured in seconds (or less, in the case of high-frequency trading). It is important to remember that, after hundreds of thousands of tests, using a multitude of trading scenarios, I have come to know that being a long-term investor one-week-at-a-time is extremely important. Looking at the market on a weekly basis removes a LOT of emotional swings and noise out of the market. As such, I measure trends in terms of weeks...not days; not hours; not minutes and definitely not seconds.

I look for "break-out" trends, where the market moves from inside the Transition Zone to above the Zone; or conversely, when the market moves from inside the Zone to below it. These break-outs signify major changes in "investment bias".

The next major trend that comes into play is "how the market is trending when it is above, inside or below the Transition Zone. The following are the rules for using the Transition Zone to set the proper investment bias:

1. As long as the market is inside the Transition Zone, the investment bias is neutral, which means you are looking to go to cash at any opportunity (i.e., stop outs, selling long positions, covering short positions).
2. When the market moves from inside the Transition Zone to above the Zone, the investment bias turns bullish.
3. When the market moves down for more than two consecutive weeks when above the Zone, the investment bias remains bullish, but new positions are not added to the portfolio. When I am buying new positions, I want the market above the Zone AND trending higher on a week-over-week analysis.
4. When the market moves below the Transition Zone, the investment bias moves from neutral to bearish, which means you are looking for opportunities to short the market.
5. Just like when the market is above the Zone, the inverse is true when the market is below the Zone. You will want to see the trend of the market moving lower when the market is below the Zone. This is the time to consider adding new short (or inverse ETFs) positions to the portfolio.

THIRD LAW
NEVER MAKE THE ASSUMPTION THAT YOU KNOW MORE THAN THE MARKET IS TELLING YOU

A corollary to the Third Law of Investing is this, "The market is never wrong!" If you believe the market is wrong, what you really have to come to grips with is: You are wrong. This is true for everyone, from the least knowledgeable to the most gifted, all-knowing analyst in the world. The market defines truth when it comes to investing. The old (very old) adage "Don't fight the tape" was right when the only way you could know what the market was doing, was by standing next to the ticker tape machine; and it is right today when information is almost instantaneously known about any market. When you find yourself on the wrong side of the market, either go to cash or switch sides.

"The market" is the collective knowledge of every trader, investment firm, analyst, pundit, financial manager, investor or investment group in the entire world. The market is *always* right, because the market is what it is. I believe that the market is always priced to perfection. I do not believe there is some magical or intrinsic "undervalued" condition that makes a stock worth more today than the level it is trading at. It may well be undervalued or overvalued when compared to where the market will be in the future, but regardless of what all the professional analysts and stock pickers say to the contrary, stocks are ALWAYS valued at exactly what they should be. The market determines the true value (intrinsic or otherwise) of a stock and not a penny more or a penny less.

Don't get me wrong—you can always 'guess' that a stock or the market as a whole, will be lower next week or higher next month. And, sometimes you can guess right. I make it a policy to never put my money or my clients' money to work in the stock market based on a guess…not anyone's guess.

But you must be asking, "Then how do you know what to buy, when to buy and when to sell?" Refer to the First Law: The Current Trend WILL Continue Until It Doesn't.

The answer is simple: Don't buy any equity if the market is trending against you. *Never buy any equity if the market is not supporting your trade.* I cannot over emphasize this statement: The key to improving your ability to make consistent profits in the stock market should be completely governed by knowing what the market <u>is doing</u>; and NOT what you think it will be doing in the future.

You can buy the best stock in the world, but if the broader market is moving into a bear cycle, the odds of that great stock improving in share price will be significantly diminished.

As such, I only want you to buy equities when the market is in an uptrend. The opposite is true for down-trending markets. I only want to short (or buy inverse ETFs) when the market is in a down-trend.

STOP GUESSING

Every analyst, financial talking head, or financial advisor who tells you anything about the future market is just guessing. I just read a news article that said, "Warren Buffet's Value Investing strategy is now back in vogue." Sounds like a reasonable approach to buying a stock, doesn't it? Not in my world it isn't!

Allow me to translate the above definition of Value Investing: "Value investing is an investment strategy based purely on guessing." You could guess right or you could guess wrong, but regardless of how you look at it, any type of investing strategy that is based on how the market will or will not reward investors with higher (or lower) share prices in the future, is just a guess. It does not matter if you want to be a value investor, a momentum investor, a low PE investor, a fundamental investor or a technical investor. If you make your decisions about what to buy, when to buy and when to sell, based on an assumption about the future, your money is at significantly higher risk. You can dramatically lower that risk if you buy when the current trend of the market is supporting your trade. *You should buy based on math. You should sell based on math. You should NEVER buy or sell based on a guess!*

AND ABOVE ALL ELSE…YOU MUST BE WILLING TO SELL AND CUT YOUR LOSSES WHEN THE MARKET MOVES AGAINST YOU. DO NOT LET YOURSELF BE SUCKERED INTO FURTHER LOSSES SIMPLY BECAUSE YOU DO NOT WANT TO SELL.

Do NOT listen to or follow anyone or any strategy that is based on a set of assumptions that must prove to be completely accurate in the future to be successful. Yes, you 'could' argue that my statement that the current trend will continue until it doesn't is an assumption about the future, but it is not. The current trend will continue until "it doesn't" is a mathematical fact and not an assumption or hope. Do

NOT invest your money in the stock market based on guesses of any kind. There is no need to guess…not ever! You need to come to this realization: "You can know with 100% certainty, how long the current trend of the market will be. It will last exactly until it doesn't." Buy when the market is bullish. Go to cash when the market is in transition. Put on short trades when the market is bearish. It is a simple concept and a profound one.

Yes…You CAN know, how long a current trend will last…100% of the time.

You may be thinking, "Oh boy…Mike's really lost it here. How silly that statement is!"

If you are thinking this way, you would be wrong. This concept of a trend continuing until it doesn't is one of the most profoundly important truisms you can find in investing money in the stock market.

Let me explain…

Let's assume the market has been trending higher, for the most part, for the last several months; even years, as it is at this writing. Everyone knows this current bull market trend will not last forever, but it has lasted a long, long time and all indications are that there is nothing on the horizon to stop it from continuing to climb higher and higher. This past Friday, the market hit another lifetime highest high.

But, here is what I know mathematically: All bear market corrections start at a market top.

Maybe last Friday was the very top of the market and now the next major bear market is underway.

How will you know when a bear market will begin? You won't.

But, you will know when one is in play. What is more, you will know when the current bull market *has ended* (please note, "has ended" is in past tense).

Here is how you will know when the bull market has ended and the 'potential' of a bear market has begun:

- A new trend is in play that can be mathematically measured. You can look back at the market and see when it started (not will start, but when it started, again, past tense).
- How do you recognize that a new trend has started? Answer: When a new market trend is moving in the opposite direction of the bull market trend.
- To determine a new trend is in play, you have to know the difference between market volatility and a change in trend. I am going to show you how to know this in a bit, but here is a hint: A new trend reversal has begun when the market enters the Transition Zone, either from below the Zone or from above the Zone.

A bull market will end when the market moves from above the Transition Zone to inside the Zone. The same is true for knowing when a bear market has ended. A bear market will end when the market moves from below the Transition Zone to inside the Zone.

When the market is trading inside the Transition Zone, the market is considered to be "in transition."

SEEING HOW THIS WORKS A DECADE AT A TIME

So far, I have only provided you with explanations, definitions and my opinion about the efficacy of a market-directional approach to growing and protecting your investable net worth. Perhaps you would like a little more "proof" that this methodology works in any reasonable timeframe. Anyone can (and many do—John Bogle is a master at this) pick a start and end date to 'prove' whether or not an investment strategy works or does not work. But, I have never seen anyone attempt to prove the efficacy of an investment strategy based solely on arbitrary begin and end dates. Appendix C provides a series of performance charts of the S&P 500 by decade; starting in 1950 with no special start/stop dates. In these charts you will see how my Market-Directional Investing Methodology compares to buy-and-hold.

How to Know When to Have a Bullish, Neutral or Bearish Investment Bias

By this point, you clearly understand that I am a firm believer in letting the trend of the market dictate your investment bias, which can be ONLY one of the following:

- Bullish and Trending Higher
- In Transition
- Bearish and Trending Lower

And, you have seen enough charts (refer to Appendix C) to know that the market is either above, inside or below the "Transition Zone". It is this Transition Zone that I want to focus on at this point.Since the beginning of the stock market there have been many attempts by technical traders to find a line or point of demarcation that would signify or precipitate a trade decision, which can only be: buy, sell or hold. I list many of these technical methodologies in the "Technicals Trading Rule". It is likely you are using or have used one or more of the popular ones at some point in your investing lifetime.

Don't get me wrong, there are many fine technical methodologies that utilize very sound principles for specific equities to buy, sell or hold. There are a few that even try to tell you things like when the market is overbought or oversold. But markets can remain overbought or oversold for long, long periods of time. It is vitally important that you know whether you should in a bullish, neutral or bearish investment mindset. Once you know this, you can go about making trading and investment decisions accordingly.

THE TURNER MARKET-BIAS INVESTMENT CONCEPT...
HOW TO PUT IT TO WORK:

This book is intended to provide you with a methodology that will help you achieve better results in your stock market investing. Let's start with Figure 2, below:

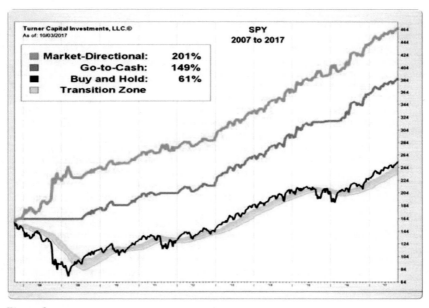

Figure 2

In this chart, I show you the S&P 500 as represented by the SPY ETF between the years of 2007 and 2017. The bottom, black line, is the week-ending closing price of the SPY. The yellow band that follows along this line is the 200-day moving average of the SPY and is called the Transition Zone. It is the 200-day moving average of the SPY, plus or minus one standard deviation of normal volatility (see the Stop Loss Trading Rule to learn how to calculate this value).

After extensive back-testing and thousands of real-world trades, I have come to the following conclusions:

1. The Transition Zone provides an excellent indication of when the market is "In Transition", which is when the market is moving from a bullish condition to a bearish condition or from a bearish condition to a bullish condition.

2. When the market is trading inside this Zone, there are not enough clear trend indications to determine whether the market is bullish, neutral or bearish. As such, the market is at its highest level of uncertainty (riskiest) when it is inside this Zone.

3. Once the market moves above this Zone, it has a historical tendency to stay above the Zone for considerable periods of time; sometimes years, even decades. As such, when the market moves above the Transition Zone, the market is considered to be bullish and that means, by extension, the mindset of the investor should be bullish.

4. Once the market moves below the Transition Zone, it has a historical tendency to stay below the Zone for extended periods of time; sometimes many months to a few years. As such, when the market moves below the Zone, the market is considered to be bearish and means, by extension, the mindset of the investor should be bearish.

5. As mentioned above, the riskiest time to be in the market is when the market is inside the Transition Zone. Here is why:

When the market is above the Zone, the likely direction of the market is in a bullish direction. Likewise, when the market is below the Zone, the likely direction of the market is in a bearish direction.

However, when the market is inside the Transition Zone, there is little historical precedent to indicate a likely direction of the market. It could just as easily move up as down. If you have to guess what the market is going to do, the best course of action is to move to cash. Guessing is not a good investment strategy. This is why, my Market-Directional Methodology always moves to cash when the market is trading inside the Transition Zone.

By the time the market has moved from below the Transition Zone, to inside the Zone, to above the Zone, a very clear bullish trend is in play. In such times, it makes sense to have a bullish investment bias. Likewise, when the market moves from above the Transition Zone, to inside the Zone, to below the Zone, a very clear bearish trend is in play. In these times, it makes sense to have a bearish investment bias.

With my Market-Directional Methodology, all trading decisions and trading biases are triggered from where the market IS in relation to the Transition Zone. Below is how this Zone is used in the practical application of the methodology:

1. When the market (in this example, the SPY) moves into the Transition Zone from above the Zone, stops that have not been triggered are adjusted high and tight against current holdings only if those holdings are moving higher; otherwise, the open positions are sold.

2. When the market moves into the Transition Zone from below the Zone, stops that have not been triggered are adjusted low and tight against the current short holdings only if those holdings are moving lower; otherwise, the shorts are covered.

3. The objective for an actively managed portfolio of equities is to be 100% cash by the time the market exits the Transition Zone, either to the upside or the downside.

4. If the market moves from inside the Zone to above the Zone, the following "legging in" rules apply:

   a. The first week, 10% of capital is invested in fundamentally strong, technically up-trending equities (see Trading Rules that follow this Chapter).

   b. The next week's weekending close of the market MUST BE higher than the previous week's weekending close in order to put another 15% to 20% into fundamentally strong, technically up-trending equities. Otherwise, no additional capital is put to work in new positions. This process continues iteratively until 100% of capital is invested or, in rare instances, the market returns to inside the Transition Zone.

5. If the market moves from inside the Zone to below the Zone, the following legging in rules apply:

   a. The first week, 10% of capital is invested in up-trending ETFs or shorting technically and fundamentally weak equities (see Trading Rules).

   b. The next week's weekending close of the market MUST BE lower than the previous week's weekending close in order to put another 15% to 20% into short-biased equities. Otherwise, no additional capital is put to work in new positions. This process continues iteratively until 100% of capital is invested or, in rare instances, the market returns to inside the Transition Zone.

Summary:

The take-away's from this Chapter are simple and straightforward:

1. The market will continue on its present trend until it doesn't.

2. The market is either in a bullish, transition or bearish condition.

3. When the market is above the Transition Zone, the market is considered bullish.

4. When the market is below the Transition Zone, the market is considered bearish.

5. When the market is inside the Transition Zone, the market is considered to be in transition.

6. Never put money into the market by buying any equity in a long position if the market is not bullish and trending higher.

7. Never short any equity if the market is not bearish and trending lower.
8. Work your way to cash when the market is inside the Transition Zone.

MOVING FORWARD:

By this point in your reading, you should know that if the market is not above the Transition Zone AND trending higher, you do not want to even look at any equity to buy. As long as the market is not above the Transition Zone and trending higher, you need not be thinking about what to buy or looking at potential stocks to buy or considering any equity to buy. Buying is off the table when the market is not above the Transition Zone and trending higher.

The following chapters ONLY come into play when the market is above the Transition Zone and trending higher (or for those of you who like to play the short side, when the market is below the Transition Zone and trending lower).

Each chapter is a different rule to use when narrowing the list of equities that you will finally decide to buy. But, you are wasting your time to use these rules to find a stock to buy if (repeating!) "the market is not above the Transition Zone and trending higher."

It is critically important that you read each of the Trading Rules that follow this chapter and to be ready to use them when the time is right, according to where the market is in relation to the Transition Zone.

In "The Right Investment Bias Rule", you have the actionable conditions to invoke before buying or shorting any equity. In "The Fundamentals Rule", you find how to score a stock's fundamentals. In "The PE Rule", you find how to appropriately use the PE of a stock to determine its relative value within its peer group. "The Technicals Rule" is all about how to score a stock's technicals and how to avoid technically weak stocks. "The Stop Loss Rule" is one of the most important rules in this book (next to the first Rule) and it gives you the formula to calculate stop loss setting using normal volatility. "The Anti-Emotion Rule" covers how damaging emotion can be to being a successful trader. "The Insider Buying Rule" deals with how to use insider buying to give you an edge on potential future movements of a stock's share price. "The Institutional Ownership Rule" is a great rule for tapping into what the big institutions are buying and selling. "The Asset Allocation Rule" is all about how to stay properly diversified.

There is no magic to consistently generating a profitable stock portfolio. It takes work, rules, and above all else, discipline. This book contains the rules and methodology for applying those rules in an actively managed stock portfolio, but you must supply the discipline to follow these rules. I cannot overemphasize that putting capital at risk in the stock market when the market is not supporting your risk exposure is the formula for failure and substantial loss of capital. However, the opposite is true as well. If you only put capital at risk when the market is supporting your risk exposure, you will enjoy more financial success and at far less risk than you ever thought possible. You will learn why a market directional approach to asset management produces far higher returns at far lower risk than any buy-and-hold strategy or any market-timing strategy.

This is a How-To book that gives you the exact formula for success. All you have to do is to put it to the test. Put it to work. You will be glad you did!

CHAPTER 2

THE FUNDAMENTALS RULE

"If you are going to own a stock . . .
it should be a good one!"

UPWARD TRENDING TECHNICALS +
STRONG DEMAND FUNDAMENTALS =
INVESTMENT SUCCESS

This Rule is "How to think like a fundamentalist." It is all about stock selection. It could be titled the "*What* to *Consider* Buying" rule. Reducing your universe of stocks to only fundamentally strong companies will lower your risk and improve your chances of generating significant and consistent profits. In this rule, you will learn why *thinking* like a fundamentalist is good, but *trading* like a fundamentalist is bad. In this rule, you will learn how to know *what* to *consider* buying, not *when* to buy. You will learn *when* to buy in the Technicals Rule.

You will learn the importance of stock selection based on some, but not all, fundamentals. You may know a lot about fundamental analysis, or you may have no idea what the term means. Regardless, this is a must-read rule. Don't rush through it, and certainly do not skip it. This is a critically important rule.

When you learn the concept of thinking like a fundamentalist, you will be surprised at how easy and straightforward it is to use that thinking to vastly improve your ability to know just the right stocks to "consider" buying. The key is to own *only* fundamentally strong stocks, but you want to own them *only at the right time.*

You may already use fundamentals in your analysis of a company before buying the stock. If you do, that is good. If you don't, you soon will. Remember, half of your decision making about what to buy is based on fundamentals. The other half is based on technicals, which we will get into in later rules.

Keep this concept in your mind throughout this book: You want to develop a set of rules that will give you a distinct advantage in the stock market. This doesn't mean you have to become a master of everything there is to know about fundamental analysis or technical analysis. In fact, you are better off not becoming too consumed with too much analysis. You could spend dozens (even hundreds) of hours studying a company's fundamentals before you buy stock in that company. But, unless you are a Warren Buffett, where you are buying millions of shares, you really do not have to spend all that much time in your fundamental analysis.

This may seem somewhat counterintuitive. After all, if an investment methodology is good enough for Warren Buffett why wouldn't it be good enough for any investor? It all comes down to the law of diminishing returns.

As an engineer, I am always looking for the most efficient use of my time. I want to spend the least amount of time possible to extract the minimum level of information required to make an appropriately informed decision about the quality of the fundamentals of a stock.

LAW OF DIMINISHING RETURNS

This "law" has as its premise that there is a point at which the cost of obtaining additional knowledge becomes significantly higher than the value of knowledge itself. In other words, the effort you would have to expend to find enough additional knowledge about a company will cost you much more than the investment you are making in the company. For a stockholder who is only buying a small fraction of a company's total outstanding shares, the cost of significant additional fundamental research becomes far more expensive than the shareholder will ever hope to make in net total return. Warren Buffett, however, can spend significant effort and cost to analyze every aspect of a company's fundamentals and have very little negative impact on his potential net total return.

If you spend too little effort, you will not have the sufficient information to make an intelligently informed decision. This means that you would be putting too much faith in your hunches or what you hear on TV every evening or what your broker told you or what your golfing buddy said. You must do your own fundamental research, and you must do enough to make an intelligent and informed opinion, but don't overdo this research.

Don't spend too much effort, though. Too much research on a company can lead you to buy the company's stock because you have invested so much of your time researching it. You will begin to justify the purchase of stock because, either consciously or subconsciously, you have already invested so much of your valuable time that you will want to justify that effort by owning shares in the company. That is overkill on research. And, don't spend more time researching the fundamentals than it is worth. A little later in this rule, I will give you a list of fundamentals that are easy to research and give you just the right amount of business knowledge of the company to justify making a stock selection decision.

Your Rights as a Shareholder

I often find that investors think they are actually buying a piece of a company when they buy the stock of that company. Some even think that when they pay their broker for those shares, somehow the company is selling the shares and that the money they paid for the shares actually flows directly back to the company. Both of these assumptions are completely false. Remember, when you buy shares of a company, you are buying *only* a tiny fraction of the outstanding publicly traded shares. Buying shares of a company does not mean money flows from you to the company...unless you are buying shares of an IPO (Initial Public

Offering). All you did was buy some pieces of paper that someone else wanted to sell you. Your money flowed from you to the person selling their shares and not to the company.

It is true that shareholders are typically granted special privileges, including the right to vote on matters such as elections to the board of directors and the right to share in distributions of the company's income, assuming the company, of its own volition, actually distributes income. However, shareholders' rights to a company's assets are subordinate to the rights of the company's creditors. What this really means is that you do not actually own a piece of the company's assets as a shareholder. Do you doubt this? Okay, the next time a company is getting ready for bankruptcy, buy one share and see what you get on the other side of the bankruptcy event. The *only* time you are likely to get anything is when the company goes out of business and liquidates its assets and owes its creditors less than its liquidated value. That almost never happens. What happens, most of the time, is that the company reorganizes under the bankruptcy laws and then issues new stock to new shareholders. The previous shareholders are left with absolutely nothing—no shares, no assets, no refunds, no shares in the new company, nothing. So don't kid yourself; if you own shares of stock in a company, all you really own are pieces of paper that are bought and sold on stock exchanges based on simple supply-and-demand market forces. Why is this important to know? It is important because I don't want you to get emotionally tied to a company via its stock. Keep in mind that a share of stock is really nothing more than a derivative of the company.

There is a misconception that when you buy a share of stock, the money that you pay somehow filters its way back to the company that issued the stock. It does not. This happens *only* when you are a part of the original or subsequent public offering. Once the shares start trading after the public offering event, you are participating in a market where the public is buying and selling shares strictly between the owner and the seller of pieces of paper. If the price of a company's stock quadruples in price, the company does not get one dime of that increase unless it issues new shares. Of course, the people who work for the company, including the corporate management, will own shares of the company and they will, just like any other shareholder, enjoy the increase in value of their shares. But the company itself does not get *any* additional cash from the shares that are being traded (bought and sold) on the open market.

DERIVATIVE

In very general terms, a derivative is just something (in this case, a share of stock) whose value changes in response to the changes in underlying variables (in this case, the company that issued the stock).

This is often confusing when you hear the financial talking heads discuss "market cap." If the market price of a stock drops by 20%, for example, you will hear the financial analysts talking about how the company's market cap was suddenly cut by 20%, resulting in the fact that the company is now worth so many billion dollars less than it was the day before, or words to that effect. In reality, nothing changed as far as the company is concerned. The actual business operations, the book value, the revenue, the total sales, the products in the pipeline, and the like did not change one iota just because the share price dropped by 20%. That 20% change was the change in the total worth of all the publicly traded shares of the company. And who owns those shares? Investors do, not the company. So it is the collective group of investors that lost their market cap, not the company. There *is* an exception to this:

When a company uses the stock it owns of its own company as collateral for loans, and then the share price drops, its collateral also drops in value. This can cause a company to experience significant financial distress if that company had its stock highly leveraged (i.e., collateralized).

Remember, you are just buying and selling pieces of paper that have value only because someone else (another investor) is willing to pay you a certain amount of money for those shares.

The objective of this rule is to teach you how to incorporate a fundamental analysis into your investment strategy and save a lot of time by concentrating on only a small subset of fundamentals that are the most important to consider when you are looking for just the right stock.

MARKET CAP

A measurement of corporate or economic size that is equal to the current market share price x the number of shares outstanding.

OBJECTIVE

There are several thousand stocks that trade every day in markets all over the world, with over 158,000 at this writing, that trade just on U.S. exchanges alone. When you get ready to add a stock to your portfolio, your objective is to pick the right stock out of this vast sea of publicly traded companies.

But the selection process of trying to pick just the right stock from such a large universe of stocks can be a daunting task. It can seem like you are trying to find a needle in a haystack. Actually, this analogy is true. But in this rule, you will learn that finding that needle (or perfect stock, in our case) is far simpler than you might think.

The first step is to understand that fundamentals really do matter when it comes to finding that perfect stock. But an exhaustive study of a company's fundamentals can be overwhelming and very time consuming. Fortunately, there are very few fundamentals that really matter when you are trying to find just the right stock to consider buying.

FUNDAMENTALS DO MATTER—
JUST NOT ALL OF THEM

To start this process, I want you to *think like a fundamentalist*. Perhaps you are unfamiliar with the term as it is used in stock analysis and don't know what it means to be a fundamentalist, let alone think like one. But, before I explain what it means to think in this way, I would like to share a story with you:

> *At a recent World Money Show, a lady came strolling by the booth, with her eyes cast upward toward the 20-foot banner that spread across the top of our booth. Across the right side it said, "Think like a Fundamentalist," and on the left side, it*

said, "Trade like a Technician." She stopped and pointed up at the sign and asked in a rather indignant tone, "Just what are you trying to say with that statement up there?" We turned to look at the sign and asked her which statement she wanted clarified. The lady said, "It's that 'think like a fundamentalist.' Are you telling me I have to be a Christian to invest in the stock market? You need to rethink the way you do your marketing!" Before we could respond, the lady walked off.

Suffice it to say, in the context of this book, the term *Fundamentalist* is someone who examines a company's financials and operations—such as sales, earnings, growth potential, assets, debt, management, products, and competition—for the sole purpose of determining if the company's fundamentals meet the fundamentalist's requirements.

A fundamentalist, then, is anyone who makes a stock investment decision based, at least in part, on the results of analysis of the company's financial condition.

FUNDAMENTALIST

With regard to the stock market, a fundamentalist is someone who uses a company's financials and operations to make trading decisions.

This analysis is called *fundamental analysis*. Investors who rely heavily on a fundamental analysis to determine what and when they trade in the stock market are considered *fundamental investors*.

Table 2.1 shows a reasonably exhaustive list of fundamentals.

As you can see, this list of fundamentals can be overwhelming. You could spend many hours researching a company based on these fundamentals before making your decision to buy. Then each time new information comes out on the company, you would have to reanalyze the company again, using all of these fundamental parameters. This would consume many more hours. But you will find that you need to study only a few of these fundamentals to learn all you need to make a stock selection decision. I call this small subset of fundamentals my "Demand Fundamentals." I'll explain more about this smaller subset a little later in the rule.

Nevertheless, think about how much time you would need to spend working on all these fundamentals if you just have 10 stocks in your portfolio. But, what if you have 20 or 30 or more? This could rapidly become way more than a full-time job. You might even have to consider hiring a few MBA graduates to help you!

Faced with this task, far too many investors either ignore fundamentals altogether or they spend way too much time analyzing too many fundamentals. *I would never buy a stock without analyzing the company's fundamentals,* but I am interested in only a very discrete few fundamentals. If your goal is to buy only stocks that will move up in price, you will want to analyze those parameters that have the biggest impact on driving stock prices higher or lower.

Remember, you are using a fundamental analysis to find those stocks that you will *consider* buying. You should **never** buy a stock solely based on a fundamental analysis. There are just too many other factors that come into play when picking a stock to buy. My 10 rules in this book will teach you how, what, and when to buy and how, what, and when to sell. Using fundamental analysis as the only criterion to buy a stock means you are leaving way too much to luck that your stock selections will make you money. I don't buy stocks and hope I am going to be lucky. I make money in the stock market because of the 10 rules in this book, not because of luck. I would rather you become a disciplined, thoughtful, smart investor. Plus, you will find that the more you follow a well-thought-out investment strategy based on a solid set of rules, the "luckier" you will become at making money—serious money—in the stock market.

At the beginning of the previous paragraph, I used the word *consider.* It is critically important that you realize the fundamentals rule is used only to find those stocks that you should "consider" buying when the time is right. This rule will help you determine *what to buy,* not *when to buy.* You will learn *when to buy* in the technicals rule and above all else, whether the market supports the trade, which you learned in Chapter 1 (Market Directional Investing. When you learn the concept of thinking like a fundamentalist, you will be surprised at how easy and straightforward it is to use that thinking to vastly improve your ability to select (not buy) the right stocks at the right time.

Table 2.1 General Fundamentals

Total cash	Insider shares sold
Profit margin	Shares held by institutions
Operating margin	Number of institutions holding shares
Debt to equity	Price-to-sales (PS) ratio
Last split ratio	Revenue per share
Trailing price-to-earnings (PE) ratio	Revenue per employee
Forward PE ratio	Net income per employee
Last year's PE ratio	Year-over-year revenue
Trailing PS ratio	Quarter-over-quarter revenue
Last year's PS ratio	Year-over-year earnings
Market cap	Dividend rate
Annual dividend	5-year average dividend
Current dividend	5-year revenue growth rate
Payout ratio	3-year revenue growth rate
Yield	5-year annual income growth rate
Current earnings per share (EPS)	3-year annual income growth rate
Forecast earnings per share	5-year dividend growth rate
Earnings before interest, taxes, depreciationand amortization (EBITDA)	3-year dividend growth rate
Total revenue	Gross margin
Total outstanding shares	Price-to-book ratio
Total shares short	Book value per share
Insider percentage	Last 3 quarters' EPS growth rate
Current inventory	Annual EPS growth rate
Previous year's inventory	5-year average EPS
Institution percentage	5-year EPS growth rate
Return on equity	Price strength
Previous year's net profit	Industry ranking
Total employees	Sector ranking
Short interest ratio	Product pipeline
Short interest percent of float	Competitive advantage
Insider shares bought	

The key is only to own fundamentally strong stocks, but you want to own them only at the right time.

So with all this in mind, let's dig in to the nitty-gritty of why fundamentals are important and how to best use them to make stock selection decisions.

Why Risk Can Be Mitigated with Strong Fundamentals

To make consistent profits in the stock market, it is important to consistently measure *net total return* against the *risk* you had to take to make that return. All of us want to make the highest return possible for the lowest risk possible. One way to keep risk low is to only own stocks that have the strongest fundamentals. In general, the stronger the fundamentals of a company, the less risk there is that the company will go bankrupt or abruptly change from being very profitable to being very unprofitable.

Also, stocks with strong fundamentals tend to have lower volatility or beta. Lower volatility generally means more consistent and predictable trends in share price movement. High-quality companies with strong fundamentals also tend to pay higher dividend yields and/or have stronger buyback programs, which add to shareholder value.

By analyzing a company's fundamentals, an investor should be able to make an informed decision about whether buying the company's stock is a good investment or a bad investment. In our case, we want to analyze a company's Demand Fundamentals so that we can make an intelligent, informed decision regarding the merits of owning shares of stock in that company.

Risk

The likelihood of a stock's price dropping low (perhaps to zero) can be tied somewhat to the stock's (actually the company behind the stock) volatility (pricing movement) over time. Risk can be extremely subjective and its measurement can depend significantly on the "risk tolerance" of each individual. Risk can be measured quantitatively as well. In this regard, one can generally assume that the higher the quality of a stock's fundamentals, the lower the likelihood that the stock's price will go to zero. On an individual stock basis, risk can be measured by comparing the stock's beta, which is a measure of the stock's volatility in relation to the rest of the market. Risk can also be mitigated or reduced through the use of diversification by industry and sector (see The Diversification Rule in Chapter 9). Further, risk can be limited through the use of stop losses (see The Stop Loss Rule in Chapter 5).

We also make a giant leap of faith that analyzing a company's fundamentals provides us with an indication of how strong the company will be in the future. We want to own stock in a company that has the likelihood of strong future growth. We use the fundamental data published by public companies as an indicator of how well the company has done in the recent past, how it compares to its peer group, and how well it will do in the future. It is this future that most interests us.

BETA

A statistical measure of the relative volatility of a publicly traded equity in comparison to the overall market. The beta for the market is considered to be 1.00. Equities, such as stocks, with betas above 1.0 tend to move with the market, but to a greater degree. Equities with a beta below 1.0 tend to move against or in the opposite direction of the overall market. For example, if the market moves up 10%, a stock with a beta of 4 will move up 40%, but a stock with a beta of 0.9 will move down 10% in that same market.

SHAREHOLDER VALUE

The equity portion of a company's capitalization, which is determined by multiplying the number of outstanding shares by current share price.

Knowing how a company has performed in the past is important, but not nearly as important as knowing how a company will perform in the future. Fundamental analysts always use past performance as a guide of future performance. It is this "future performance" that we buy when we buy shares of stock in a company.

Unfortunately, fundamentals tend to be very lagging indicators. For example, the fact that a company reports that it beat street expectations does not necessarily guarantee that it will repeat that feat in the upcoming quarter.

The best you can do with a fundamental analysis is to use the results to compare one company to another or one company to a group (industry, sector, or the entire market) of companies. If you can determine that the fundamentals of a company are improving, and perhaps improving more rapidly than its peers, you can reasonably conclude that the company's stock is potentially worth owning.

It is important to get the most reliable fundamental data available. Investors generally turn to publicly available financial reports, such as the annual 10K and quarterly 10-Q reports, where the actual performance of the company is spelled out in black and white. The numbers don't lie—or at least they shouldn't—and can be used as a basis for making investment decisions.

LAGGING INDICATORS

Information or trends that provide historical trends or accomplishments, but do not predict future events.

STREET EXPECTATIONS

The average estimates made by brokers and securities analysts regarding various components (generally revenue and earnings) of a company's fundamentals.

Keep in mind that even the most recently released reports contain data that are very lagging to the actual operation of the company. By the time a 10-K or 10-Q is published, the company is making material operational decisions that are months, if not years, ahead of the data in these reports. While quarterly and annual reports serve as excellent references of where the company has been, they do little to tell you where the company is going.

When you buy stock in a company, the future share price of that stock is directly tied to the future of the company, not its past.

But as lagging as fundamentals are, they still provide an important measuring stick of how well the company has performed over time and in comparison to its peers.

10-K

A Securities and Exchange Commission (SEC)-required and audited annual report that contains the financial results of the company for the past 12 fiscal months.

10-Q

An SEC-required document that contains the financial results of the company for the quarter, noting any significant changes or events. Usually, but not always, companies will also release forecasts on the expected financial results of future quarters, generally not more than one year into the future.

WHY I AM NOT A FUNDAMENTAL PURIST

I would like to sidestep for a minute to express my differences with the pure fundamentalists, if I may. I am not sure where to delve into this subject, but perhaps now is the best time.

This next statement is not an opinion—it is a fact: The fundamentals of a company do not have anything directly to do with the price of shares of stock for that company.

That statement may surprise you, and for the pure fundamentalists out there, to say that strong fundamentals have nothing to do with the share price of a stock seems ludicrous. They would argue that share price and a company's fundamentals are inextricably connected, that, in fact, there is no other real way to determine share price.

I completely understand this line of reasoning, and on the surface it does seem logical. But if all it took for the share price of a stock to go up was for the company to have strong fundamentals, then ask yourself this question: Why does the price of a company's stock sometimes go down even when the fundamentals have not changed?

If the change in share price is tied only to the quality of the stock's fundamentals, then:

- Investors would only buy stocks with strong fundamentals.
- The share price of fundamentally strong companies would always go up.
- Investors would never lose money on a stock as long as the stock's fundamentals continued to be strong.

This, of course, is absolutely not what happens. The share price of fundamentally strong stocks often does drop in price, sometimes precipitously!

My argument with the fundamental purists is this: since the share price of fundamentally strong companies often moves lower, then higher, and then lower again, without the fundamentals of the company changing, then you cannot rely on fundamentals alone in stock selection.

So just what *does* make the share price of a stock move up or down? Let's look and see.

AND NOW A LITTLE PHYSICS LESSON

Newton's first law of physics is, "A body in motion tends to stay in motion unless acted upon by an outside force." Now, before your eyes glaze over, this physics lesson is merely to illustrate the importance of strong fundamentals.

Stay with me here—this concept is important. You see, we (you and I) investors have one primary objective (or should have) with regard to investing in the stock market. That objective is to make consistent profits. The problem is: *How* do we achieve that objective?

To solve this problem, the solution is simple: Sell stocks at a higher price than you buy them. Okay, now that we have the problem and the solution, we need to make sure the process used actually gets us to our objective.

Basically, that process (or investment methodology) is to buy stocks at lower prices and hold onto them long enough for them to gain in share price, and then sell them before they retreat back to lower prices.

It follows, then, that if we buy a stock that is moving higher in price, we want that stock to remain in that upward pricing movement long enough for us to achieve our primary objective, which is to sell it before it turns against us and moves lower.

One of the aspects of stocks and their market pricing trends is that the stronger the stock's fundamentals, the harder it is for it to suddenly reverse its upward pricing trend.

Think of it this way: If you consider a stock with superb fundamentals to be a battleship and a stock with weak fundamentals to be a dinghy, and both are headed from lower left to upper right, which one would be easier to turn into a movement from upper left to lower right? You are right—it is the dinghy. A dinghy can turn on a dime; a battleship takes many miles to get it to change direction.

So it is with stocks. **The stronger the fundamentals of a stock, the more stable its pricing trend, the more predictive its direction, and the easier it is to make money by capitalizing on those trends.** So stick with stocks that have the stronger fundamentals. This strategy will tend to generate more consistent profits through more predictable pricing trends.

SUPPLY AND DEMAND—THE *ONLY* REASON WHY STOCK PRICES FLUCTUATE

At any given time in the market, there will be a host of stocks with share prices that are trending lower. Some of these stocks will have incredibly strong fundamentals. For example, it is not uncommon for you to find 200 to 300 stocks with very strong fundamentals, but only a few of them have share prices that are climbing. *Your objective is to buy only fundamentally strong stocks when the share price is more likely to move up than down.*

Strong fundamentals do not guarantee that a stock's share price is going to trend higher in the future. Strong fundamentals are important, but strong fundamentals are not enough of an indicator for you to use to buy a stock. In fact, fundamentals have nothing, directly, to do with the share price of a stock.

Here is why.

Have you ever really thought about what makes a stock's share price move higher or lower? As simple as this may seem to you, I find that most investors don't have any idea why a stock's market price actually moves higher or lower.

They may think, wrongly, that it has to do with a stock's fundamentals, or its management team, or its products in the pipeline, or analyst upgrades and/or downgrades. In fact, none of these reasons "directly" make a stock's share price move higher or lower.

Don't get me wrong. Fundamentals do play an important role in picking the right stock to consider buying, but fundamentals do not determine share price. The company's management team does not determine share price. New products, new discoveries, new markets, and analyst upgrades or downgrades do not determine share price.

There is only one thing that can make a stock's share price move higher or lower. That one thing is directly based on the *demand for shares.* The more investors who want to own more shares, the higher the demand. The more investors who want to own fewer shares, the lower the demand. Shares of stock are just like anything else that people buy and sell. You know what I am talking about. You learned it in high school economics class. The more demand for something, the higher the price; the lower the demand, the lower the price.

It follows that if you could predict investor demand, you could predict movement in share price. If you knew that demand was going to fall off, you would correctly expect the stock's share price to move lower. Conversely, if you knew that demand was going to increase, you would correctly predict that the share price is going to move higher.

If you can consistently predict investor demand, you can consistently and accurately predict directional moves in a stock's share price.

So what drives investor demand higher or lower? Actually, there are many things that impact this "supply-and-demand" curve for stock shares, including significant geopolitical and socioeconomic news events. But, aside from the news of the day, investor demand (or the lack thereof) for stock shares can be directly tied to just a few stock fundamentals. Since these fundamentals have the most to do with investor demand for shares, I call these particular fundamentals the *Demand Fundamentals*.

Let's see what these are.

DEMAND FUNDAMENTALS: THE KEY TO STOCK SELECTION

Demand Fundamentals are just a small subset of all the "general Fundamentals" listed earlier in Table 2.1. These very special fundamentals will tell you more about a company more quickly than you might imagine. To illustrate this concept, I want you to pick one of your favorite stocks. Perhaps this is a stock you already own, one that you have previously owned, or one that you are considering buying. Next, go to Yahoo!1 and look up this stock and click on the news or headlines section. Read anything about the stock that includes information on one or more of the fundamentals listed in Table 2.1.

Now, while you are still in Yahoo!, look at the stock's chart and try to match up the date of the news and the price movement of the stock on or near those dates. See which of these fundamentals have the most impact on a change in the price of the stock.

You can spend hours and hours poring over these data, but in the end, you will find that only a relatively small set of fundamentals have the biggest impact on investor demand. Here are my Demand Fundamentals:

- Quarter-over-quarter revenue growth rate
- Quarter-over-quarter earnings growth rate
- Year-over-year revenue growth rate
- Year-over-year earnings growth rate
- Multi-Year revenue growth rate
- Multi-Year earnings growth rate
- Relative PE Ranking

- Return on equity
- Dividend yield
- Institutional Holding
- Stock Price
- Relative Fundamental Ranking

To understand why these few Demand Fundamentals are the key to finding great stocks you have to know why a change in these fundamentals will cause a direct and sometimes significant impact on investor demand.

Investors buy stocks when they believe their investment in the shares will yield a profit at some point in the future. For shares in a company to become more valuable, the company has to become more valuable. By and large, all publicly traded companies are evaluated on one overwhelming yardstick. That yardstick is "growth." If a company's earnings, revenue, return on equity, or dividend is growing steadily over time, the company is becoming more valuable over time. The more valuable a company, the more investors will demand shares in the company. Hence, the more demand for shares, the higher the share price.

No one wants to own shares in a company that has negative growth rates in revenue, earnings, return on equity, and dividend yield. Negative growth in these areas creates less demand for shares by investors. So, again, the less demand there is for shares by investors, the lower the price for shares of stock.

It is very important to understand that it is not the fundamentals themselves that are as important as the *rate of growth* (whether that rate of growth is positive or negative) of those fundamentals.

I cannot overemphasize that *growth is the key!* It is *not* the actual value of the Demand Fundamental, but rather the *rate of change* of that Demand Fundamental from one reporting period to another that we want to use in this analysis process.

Let me give you an example of what I am talking about:

Take two companies, Company A and Company B. Last year, Company A had the best fundamentals of its peer group. It generated a 10%

net profit. Company B had only a 2% net profit growth when it reported last year. From a purely fundamental analysis perspective, ignoring rates of growth, Company A is a far stronger company than Company B. The net value of each of the fundamentals was far better for Company A than Company B.

This year, Company A had another fantastic year. Once again, it had the best fundamentals of its peer group. It generated another solid 10% net profit. Company B generated only 4% net profit.

So, here is the question: With all other things being equal, which is the better company to own—Company A or Company B? If your answer is Company B, you are right!

You may be wondering why Company B is far better to own than Company A. Let me explain.

Company A had zero *growth* in net profit, whereas Company B *doubled* its net profit. Company B had a 100% growth rate in net profit—far, far better than Company A. As such, the demand for shares of Company B will almost always push the price of its shares proportionately higher than for those shares of Company A. Based on pure fundamentals (all of which are listed in Table 2.1), Company A is a far stronger and better company than Company B. But—and this is the key—*investors pay for* **growth.** So the demand for shares of Company B will be stronger than the demand for shares of Company A. As such, the share price for Company B will move higher and much more rapidly than those of Company A.

RATE OF GROWTH

Measured by comparing the change in value over time. For example, quarter-over-quarter earnings growth is calculated by subtracting last year's quarter-ending total earnings from the current year's quarter-ending total earnings and then dividing that difference by last year's quarter-ending total earnings. Here is the example in formula format:

- QELY = Quarter-ending earnings last year at this same time for the then most recent quarterly report

- QETH = Quarter-ending earnings as of the most recent quarterly report

$$Quarter - over - Quarter\ Earnings\ Growth\ Rate = \left(\frac{QETH - QELY}{QETH} \right) \times 100\%$$

HOW TO USE DEMAND FUNDAMENTALS TO FIND THE BEST STOCK

Now that you understand that Demand Fundamentals are the key fundamentals to use when evaluating a stock, the next question should be, "How do I use these Demand Fundamentals to find the best stock?"

Remember, in this Rule, you are finding *only* those stocks that, if the timing is right, would be good stocks to own. You are *not* to use Demand Fundamentals to determine when to buy, only what to buy. And, as I will remind you throughout this book, you need not spend one minute of your time analyzing anything about any company or stock or ETF if the market is not bullish and trending higher; or for shorting purposes, bearish and trending lower. The Market-Directional Methodology determines whether or not you should be spending any time whatsoever in the analysis of which equity to buy or short.

The process to find the best stocks using Demand Fundamentals couldn't be simpler.

As a reminder, below are the twelve Demand Fundamentals:

- Quarter-over-quarter revenue growth rate
- Quarter-over-quarter earnings growth rate
- Year-over-year revenue growth rate
- Year-over-year earnings growth rate
- Multi-Year revenue growth rate
- Multi-Year earnings growth rate
- Relative PE Ranking
- Return on equity
- Dividend yield
- Institutional Holding

- Stock Price
- Relative Fundamental Ranking

All you have to do is place your universe of stocks in a list, with those having the best Demand Fundamentals at the top, and those with the worst Demand Fundamentals at the bottom. The higher the growth rates, the better. The higher the return on equity, the better. The higher the dividend yield, the better.

Using an Excel spreadsheet for this task makes the process very simple. Table 2.2 shows how I would use these fundamentals in such a spreadsheet.

After preparing a worksheet similar to the one below, you only need to sort the columns to find the best stock of each Demand Fundamental.

You can take this one step further by scoring each of the Demand Fundamentals; then add up the scores, and sort from best to worst. Table 2.3 is another example of the same five stocks, but with scores instead of actual values.

Table 2.4 is the same worksheet, but sorted based according to the "Total Score" column.

It doesn't really matter what criteria you use for scoring the Demand Fundamentals, but whatever scoring criteria you use make it consistent. Then, when you sort your stocks by the total score, you can quickly determine which stocks have the best overall Demand Fundamentals.

Table 2.2 Demand Fundamental Spreadsheet Example						
Stock	Quarter-over-Quarter Revenue Growth Rate	Year-over-Year Earnings Growth Rate	Quarter-over-Quarter Earnings Growth Rate	5-Year Average Earnings Growth Rate	Return on Equity	Dividend Yield
Ticker1	50%	20%	18%	12%	20%	0%
Ticker2	−8%	10%	5%	8%	4%	4%
Ticker3	15%	100%	10%	4%	8%	1%
Ticker4	4%	22%	50%	13%	15%	0%
Ticker5	−19%	−4%	−12%	3%	1%	0%

Table 2.3 Demand Fundamental Scoring Example (Unsorted)							
Stock	Quarter-over-Quarter Revenue Growth Rate	Year-over-Year Earnings Growth Rate	Quarter-over-Quarter Earnings Growth Rate	5-Year Average Earnings Growth Rate	Return on Equity	Dividend Yield	Total Score
Ticker1	8	4	4	2	10	0	28
Ticker2	0	1	0	1	0	8	10
Ticker3	4	10	3	1	2	4	24
Ticker4	1	4	5	3	5	0	18
Ticker5	0	0	0	0	0	0	0

Table 2.4 Demand Fundamental Scoring Example (Sorted by Total Score)							
Stock	Quarter-over-Quarter Revenue Growth Rate	Year-over-Year Earnings Growth Rate	Quarter-over-Quarter Earnings Growth Rate	5-Year Average Earnings Growth Rate	Return on Equity	Dividend Yield	Total Score
Ticker1	8	4	4	2	10	0	28
Ticker3	4	10	3	1	2	4	24
Ticker4	1	4	5	3	5	0	18
Ticker2	0	1	0	1	0	8	10
Ticker5	0	0	0	0	0	0	0

The higher the total score, the better the stock's Demand Fundamentals.

Now that you have mastered the concept of scoring Demand Fundamentals, you next need to apply this to your universe of stocks. As I said at the beginning of this rule, there are many thousands of stocks that are traded on stock exchanges every day.

But, even with all of this scoring and sorting accomplished, you still have a lot of stocks in your universe—too many, most likely. Let's get this universe down to a manageable size.

REDUCING THE SIZE OF YOUR UNIVERSE

The first step in selecting a stock is to get the list of thousands of stocks down to just a handful—maybe only 30 to 100 stocks that you will concentrate on and from which you will select the one or two new stocks for your portfolio. Before you jump to the conclusion that I am insinuating that this 30 to 100 stocks are all the stocks you will ever have to consider, please understand that this exercise of narrowing down the universe of several thousand stocks to just a handful is something you will need to repeat every time you want to add a new stock to your portfolio. The ultimate, original objective of using Demand Fundamentals to score and rank your universe of stocks in order is to quickly narrow this list down to the one or two stocks that you will consider buying.

Remember, your first job is to find the few stocks out of the thousands that have the very best Demand Fundamentals. A simple and straightforward way to make this comparison is to simply score all the stocks in your universe,[2] and then sort your stocks from the highest score to the lowest score. My universe of stocks is about 6,000. I have a scoring system for each of the 12 Demand Fundamentals (see Appendix B).

When you get ready to pick the 10 or 20 stocks to have in your portfolio, the first step is to *score* your universe of stocks. Make a list of those companies that you want to consider buying shares of stock in and assign a score to each of the Demand Fundamentals for each company using the scoring system described in Appendix B.

Once you have determined the scores for each stock in your universe of stocks, the next step is to add up each of the individual scores into a total "Demand Fundamental Score." Using a scoring process gives you the ability to then rank the stocks from the highest score to the lowest.

Then sort the total Demand scores from the best to the worst. Of course, your objective is to own only the best. But, remember, the fact that a stock has the highest Demand Fundamental score does *not* mean that you should run out and buy it. Quite the contrary—all this last portion of Rule 1 does is to help you identify the companies that are the best to own.

Granted...this is a LOT of work to go through each stock and score each Demand Fundamental and then sort the list by best to worst. There is a short-cut available, though: Go to www.TurnerTrends.com where you can subscribe to the tools that I use every day. The stocks are already scored for you and all you have to do is set the criteria that you want to see a matrix of all the stocks and their Demand Fundamental scores.

And one more thing: **Don't buy any stocks yet!** You are not yet ready to buy any of these stocks you have just scored. All you have done is determine which stocks you would prefer to own *when the timing is right* to buy them.

You will learn more in subsequent Rules, but first you will need to learn how to stay clear of overpaying for a stock, which I cover in the next Rule.[1]

WHAT YOU LEARNED IN THIS RULE

You have completed "How to Think Like a Fundamentalist", where you learned:
- That you should own only stocks that are fundamentally strong.
- That a fundamental analysis tells you *what to buy,* not *when to buy.*
- That some fundamentals are more important than others when analyzing a company.
- That it is not fundamentals that make stock prices move higher or lower. Rather, it is investor demand that causes share prices to move higher or lower.
- That there are only a few fundamentals that have the largest impact on investor demand. These fundamentals are called Demand Fundamentals.

---

1 Your universe could be 20 stocks, it could be 200, or it could be all the stocks traded in the world. It all depends on how much time you can devote to doing the work required to adequately record and analyze the Demand Fundamentals of a stock.

CHAPTER 3

THE PE RULE

"Always buy more earnings with fewer dollars."

W hen you complete this book, you will be able to build your own world-class portfolio of stocks with confidence. It will be a fluid and dynamic portfolio that will change composition as the market changes. The concepts you will learn here will keep you from losing a lot of money in terrible markets and help you make a lot of money in great markets. You will know what to buy, when to buy, and, most importantly, when to sell. No more guessing—and no more sleepless nights. Chapter 1 is where you learn whether or not to be in the market at all. Chapters 2 through 10 tell you how to go about being in the market if and only if Rule 1, The Market Directional Rule, says you should be.

INDUSTRY PE IS FAR MORE IMPORTANT THAN S&P 500 PE

Before I get into the objective of this rule, let me share a quick story with you. One day, when I was about 16, I was getting ready to go out with some of my friends. Way back then (in the mid-1960s) a dollar was enough to buy some gasoline and a pretty decent meal at the local drive-in. And I was broke. So I asked my dad a question, and after his response I never asked again.

I asked, "Dad, do you have an extra dollar?" Of course, my assumption was that he would give me a dollar. But he looked at me and said, "Just what is an 'extra' dollar? I've never seen an 'extra' dollar. What does an 'extra' dollar look like? In fact, I've never even *heard* of an 'extra' dollar." He kept on and on about it. Finally, after he quit driving his point home, I restated my request. I said, "Dad, may I borrow a dollar from you?" His answer was, "Sure," and handed me a dollar for the weekend.

Not only did he drive home the fact that no money is extra and should never be considered insignificant, but that lesson also made me think about every dollar that I have earned since then. That episode in my teenage life stuck with me. Each time I would buy something, I would see those dollars in my billfold and consider the purchase from the standpoint of wise use of my money. Was this purchase being made with "extra" dollars or with important, hard-earned dollars?

So it is when you buy a stock. I don't want you wasting your money. You should spend your money very wisely when buying stocks. We are after incremental increases in profit wherever we can get those profits. One way to increase your bottom-line profit is not to pay too much for a stock when there is a better choice available.

In Rule 1, you learned how to know whether to have a bullish, neutral or bearish investment bias. In the Fundamentals Rule, you learned *what* stocks to *consider* buying. Here, in this Rule, "The Value Rule," I will show you how to choose between two stocks, if their Demand Fundamentals are identical.

In building a portfolio of high-quality stocks, you will often find that you have more great stocks to buy than you have room for in your portfolio or money with which to invest. This is a common problem that all investors face at one time or another. Think of it this way: You have two stocks that have identical Demand Fundamentals. In fact, both of these two stocks will give you the same opportunity to move higher in price. Which one will you select? In this rule, you will learn how to pick the better stock based on its relative value, thereby spending your money wisely in the process.

As the "portfolio manager" of your own personal portfolio, you are continually faced with the problem of selecting one stock from a basket of many stocks, each with great Demand Fundamentals and excellent technicals (more on this in the Technicals Rule). You will have to work through a "process of elimination" where you gradually eliminate stocks from your basket of stocks, until you have just the right one.

You will have to compare the Demand Fundamentals that you learned about in the Fundamentals Rule, the impact to diversification in the Diversification Rule, the Technicals Rule, the Institutional Owner- ship Rule, the Asset Allocation Rule, and, as you will learn in this Rule, the relative *value* of one stock over another. For this rule, *relative value* is defined by calculating how much it costs per share to buy one dollar of earnings, and then comparing one stock to another based on this relative value calculation.

A simpler way to state this is to compare the price-to-earnings (PE) ratio of one stock to the PE of another. Price divided by earnings tells you the ratio of cost of shares to the earnings derived via the owning of those shares. One of the most important measures of a company is its earnings. You learned in the Fundamentals Rule that an important com- ponent of analyzing earnings is to measure the *rate of growth in earnings*. In this Rule, you will learn how to use the combination of share price and earnings to determine which stocks have the best value. As a stock market investor, one of your objectives is not to overpay for a stock. If two stocks are equal in all other areas, it is always better to buy the one that has a better earnings value or PE.In this methodology, it is not important to only buy undervalued stocks. Quite the contrary, you may often buy relatively overvalued stocks. But when faced with a choice between two stocks that are equally weighted by their Demand Funda- mentals, you need a qualifier or criteria by which to choose one over the other. You will need to understand how to use PE ratios in order to make that decision.

When I perform this analysis, I assign a score to each stock's PE. If the stock's PE is significantly higher than the average PE for the stock's industry, I consider the stock to be overvalued. If it is near the top of its industry's PE range, I consider the stock to be highly overvalued. Likewise, if a stock is near the middle of the average PE for its industry, I consider the stock fairly valued. If it is near the bottom of its industry's PE range, I consider the stock highly undervalued. PE ratios that are between fairly valued and highly undervalued are simply undervalued.

Most fundamental based investors will consider PE ratios when analyzing a stock's fundamentals. They *wrongly* assume that a stock with a higher PE is more expensive than a stock with a lower PE. I inserted the word *wrongly* to get your attention and to make a point. Too many investors ignore a key and very important aspect of making a proper value assessment of a stock when comparing one stock to another. A little later in this rule I will show you how to avoid this error, but if you will indulge me while I sidestep for a moment to cover "Why a Value Investment Strategy Can Be Wrong For You."

Before getting into how to use value in your stock selection criteria, let me tell you what I think about being a "value investor."

When it comes to being a value investor, you must first decide how to value a company. The problem lies in being able to adequately determine real value and having access to enough of the right data to make such a determination. There are significant and polar opposite arguments on how to properly determine value and how relative it is to the current market. A lot has been written, and will continue to be written, on whether the market or a stock is overvalued or undervalued. I submit to you that, other than how I use PE ratios in the selection of stocks, it really doesn't matter whether a company, or a stock, or a sector, or an industry, or an entire market is undervalued, overvalued, or properly valued.

Value investors typically buy stocks with high dividend yields or ones that trade at a low price-to-earnings ratio (PE), or low price-to-book ratio (PB). Some famous value investors are Warren Buffett, John Templeton, John Neff, and Michael Price.

As bizarre as this may sound, I do not believe in value investing. Not that value investing is wrong. Quite the contrary—for the Warren Buffetts of the world, value investing makes a ton of sense. If you have the resources that Warren Buffett has, where you could know the inner workings of a company, its immediate and long-term prospects, the real ability of the management team, the goals of the board members, the products in the pipeline, the expected acquisitions, the real position of the company in the marketplace and/or the competitive landscape, and a hundred other very important elements associated with making a true value assessment, then, I would say you should be a value investor.

This is not to say that I don't believe in using value to help determine which stock to buy. I just don't rely exclusively on value to make my buying or selling decisions.

It is my belief that most individual investors do not have enough access to the right kinds of information to adequately be a true value investor.

Many so-called value investors try to outguess the market by using a value analysis to determine which stocks to own. Unfortunately, high-value stocks often fall precipitously in share price. These investors invariably attempt to defend why the market has improperly valued a stock when this happens. Remember, the market is never wrong. You will often hear market pundits and stock market mavens rail about how "the market has missed something" or that "the market is wrong." But I say, "The market is what it is." To be a successful stock market investor, you must work with the market, not against it. If you ever get to a point where you believe the market is wrong, it only means that you are not *in sync with the market*.

Is it important to include value in your stock selection criteria? Absolutely. But, I do not give value investing much weight when it comes to making a stock selection. My advice is to leave the bulk of value investing to the Warren Buffetts of the world. Let's stick with a much more reasonable approach that any investor can use to significantly outperform the market. You will learn how to use one simple element of value, the PE ratio, to make small but important decisions about which one, of a small handful of stocks, is better to buy when the Fundamentals Rule are the same for each stock in the group.

With regard to the market, I mentioned above that it is important to "stay in sync with the market." In the Market-Directional Methodology Chapter, I specifically defined how to ALWAYS be in sync with the market. To do otherwise means that the market has moved in the opposite direction to where you thought it was going to move. This happens when you buy a stock, assuming it is going to move higher in price, and it then moves lower in price. This also happens when you believe that an entire group of stocks (e.g., energy-related stocks) will move lower, but that group of stocks defies your logic and moves higher, thwarting your investment strategy in those stocks. When this happens, the result is all too obvious: You will lose money. The only way to make money in the stock market is to buy stocks that the market wants and to sell stocks that the market doesn't want. To make money in the stock market, you must stay in sync with the market.

What this means is this…if the market is not above the Transition Zone and trending higher, you do not want to be buying ANY security, regardless of any other consideration. I cannot overstate this to you.

Your job is not to try to determine whether a stock is properly valued, regardless of the basis used for that value determination. Your only job, as a stock market investor, is to know when to buy and when to sell. Everything else is just measuring egos and/or listening to value gurus, which is much like watching a stopped clock. It is going to be right twice a day.

However, if you have enough time and research data and can live long enough, a value theory can make some sense. But, since people don't live forever and most investors don't have nearly enough information to really determine a company's value, we are back to realizing that we should basically ignore value investing and take whatever the market is going to give us.

I *will* use value to help make a choice between two stocks with equal Demand Fundamental scores. I am, however, very much opposed to using value as the primary condition on which to make stock investment decisions.

So let me show you how to use PE ratios to help you to select the best valued stocks for your portfolio.

How to Use PE Ratios to Avoid Paying Too Much for a Stock

Most investors recognize that the lower the PE for a stock, the higher its value. In other words, the lower the PE, the less it costs you to, in effect, buy the company's earnings. And, as we learned in the previous rule, investor demand increases almost in direct proportion to a company's increasing rate of growth in earnings.

But when comparing one stock to another, you have to be very careful when using PE as a decision factor.

The key to understanding this concept can be illustrated with a candy bar and a gallon of gasoline.

If I made the following statement to you, you would think I was nuts (and you would be right): "You should buy more candy bars because one candy bar costs a lot less than one gallon of gasoline. The better value, therefore, is in the candy bar."

You know, of course, that it is ridiculous to compare candy bars to gasoline when making a purchase decision. Even if you melted the candy bar into a liquid to compare one gallon of candy bar to one gallon of gasoline, it still is an asinine comparison. Okay, then, let's compare miles per gallon. How many miles can you travel on a gallon of gasoline, as compared to the number of miles you can travel on a gallon of candy bars? I know—this is getting more and more ludicrous. Why would anyone ever make a buying decision on candy bars or gasoline by comparing the prices of the two products?

But I suspect that is *exactly* what you are doing when you use PE ratios as criteria for buying stocks when the two stocks are totally unrelated.

It is likely that you believe that comparing PE ratios is a good way to determine value, where value is the same thing as saying you are getting more for your dollar. The more earnings you can buy for the same dollar, the better. Right? Yes, that statement is true, but that does not mean you should always buy the stock with the lower PE when comparing one stock to another.

When using PE ratios to make a buying decision between two stocks that have equal or nearly equal Demand Fundamentals, you must make sure the two stocks are from the same industry. It might be reasonable to compare price per gallon of gasoline to the price per gallon of diesel when trying to make a decision on which vehicle to buy. Both of these commodities come from the same industry; in this example, they are both transportation fuels.

This probably makes some intuitive sense to you, but there is a subtlety here that I don't want you to miss.

When buying stocks, the market has determined what it believes to be "reasonable PE ranges" for a certain type (industry) of stock. Investors will buy Google for over $1,000 per share at this writing, with a PE of 18, and not bat an eye. But, JP Morgan has the exact same PE of 18, but it sells for 1/10th of what GOOG trades for. How can that be? Obviously, if your only criteria is PE, why is GOOG trading for 10 times what JPM trades for when they both have almost identical PE ratios? After all, a dollar of earnings is a dollar of earnings. What is the difference between a dollar of JPM earnings and a dollar of GOOG earnings? The answer is, "Nothing." Why, then will investors pay more for a dollar of GOOG earnings than a dollar of JPM earnings? In reality, there are a lot of reasons, but those reasons have far more to do with the potential future growth of these two companies and far less than current value.

And, sometimes, there is just not a good answer. But, still, we are just talking about what it costs to buy a dollar of earnings, which is what the PE tells us.

Here is the subtlety that I want you to grasp: The market determines acceptable and reasonable PE ranges based on nothing more than what the market will bear to pay. If the market determines that an acceptable PE range for a certain industry is 20 to 200, then a PE of 50 is not unreasonable. However, if the market has determined that an acceptable range of PE is 2 to 20 for a specific industry, a PE of 50 is completely unreasonable.

How to Avoid the PE Misconception

I have a good friend who writes a lot of articles on finance. He is often published in various journals and newspapers and on the Internet. I won't use his name for fear of either embarrassing him or receiving a bad review for my book—neither of which I want. I'll use a fictitious name for reference. I will call him "Joe."

One day, in my e-mail inbox, an article that Joe had written suddenly appeared. I like reading Joe's articles. They are almost always very insightful. In his e-mail, he was reporting on the overbought condition of the market. He was stating a lot of historical statistics on the average PE of the S&P 500. He went on and on explaining how investors were getting sucked into buying more and more expensive stocks because the average PE of the S&P 500 had moved from about 14 to over 16. He was extolling the merits of looking for stocks that had PEs in the subteens.

I was astounded at his complete disregard for the average PE by industry. He had, in one broad stroke of his pen (or, in this instance, keyboard), lumped all stocks into the same comparison criteria, where a stock that had a PE of 10 had a much better value than one of 20 or 30, regardless of its industry. As you will see, he was completely wrong in this comparison.

I wrote him about the article and pointed out what I believe is the fallacy of using the average PE of the S&P 500 as a benchmark from which to compare overvalued or undervalued conditions of equities. I expected him to be somewhat defensive, but his response to my approach to PE analysis was, "Good point."

Don't forget, your objective is to buy and sell stocks at the right time for the right price. So you should only consider buying a stock that has given you a *strong technical buy signal*, which you will learn in the Technicals Rule and has *strong Demand Fundamentals*, which you learned in the Fundamentals Rule.

Your first step is to execute the Fundamentals Rule on your universe of stocks. Executing the Fundamentals Rule means you have selected a group of stocks that pass your requirement for Demand Fundamentals.

Let's assume you have two stocks with identical Demand Fundamentals and both stocks are in the same industry, but you can buy only one of them. Now, you must choose between them. This is a situation you will encounter often. It is very common that when one stock in an industry is showing strong Demand Fundamentals, there will also be others that are just as strong.

The theory behind the PE Rule is that, with everything else being equal, comparing the PE of one stock to another is a good way to determine which stock is the better value, *so long as both stocks belong to the same industry.* Owning the stock with the better value means you are paying the least amount for the stock with the best Demand Fundamentals.

Now it is critically important that you understand that *all* of the following *must* be true:

1. **Both stocks *must* belong to the same industry.** If you break this rule, you will be wasting your time doing the rest of the comparison process.
2. You must compare the same type of PE between the two stocks. You can use a trailing PE (last 12 months), the most recently reported PE, or a forecast PE. I like to use the most recently reported PE.

For this discussion, I have selected two stocks that have (as of this writing) identical Demand Fundamentals and both belong to the electrical utilities industry. I won't use the actual ticker symbols, but will simply call them Ticker1 and Ticker2. According to their most recent quarterly reports and the then-current market price of the stocks, the PE ratios are:

- Ticker1: PE of 21.30
- Ticker2: PE of 17.40

If I could only own one of these two stocks, Ticker2 is a better value since its PE is lower. "Better value" means I can spend less money per share to get the same amount of earnings. The more earnings I can buy with fewer dollars, the better. Why? *Because earnings is one of the best metrics for evaluating the strength and growth potential of a company.* The more earnings a company makes, the better the company. Investors want to own shares in strong, growing companies. Therefore, investors look at a company's earnings and then how much it costs per share to, in effect, buy those earnings. The objective is to buy the most earnings for the fewest dollars. To know which of the two companies has the most value—meaning which of two companies has more earnings for every dollar it costs you to buy shares in those companies—all you have to do is take the current share price and divide it by the most recently reported company earnings per share (EPS). Once again, the formula is price per share divided by earnings per share equals the "PE ratio." The smaller this number, the better. Why? You want to spend the least amount possible for the most earnings possible. Why? Because the market (the entire community of people and institutions who buy and sell stock) will pay more money for more earnings. *Increasing corporate earnings* is one of the most important Demand Fundamentals.

This probably makes reasonable sense to you, but let me take you through another example. In this case, I am going to—**wrongly and without regard to industry**—select two stocks from entirely different industries (Stock A and Stock B). This, surprisingly enough, is the standard practice of most investors, where they use PE to make a value judgment on a stock, while completely ignoring the fact that the stocks come from separate industries. You see, most investors know only the average PE of the S&P 500, which at the time of this writing is about 25. Because so many of the talking heads on TV use this as some kind of magical standard from which all stocks should be compared, many investors wrongly assume that a PE lower than the average of the S&P 500 is better than a PE that is higher than the average. This misconception will get you in trouble if you let it.

Following is an example that typifies this *wrong* way of thinking about PEs.

- **Stock A** is from the Internet Information Providers Industry with a PE ratio of 50.
- **Stock B** is from the Health Care Plans Industry. It has a PE of 35.

Based on this information, which is the better stock to buy, assuming they have identical Demand Fundamentals?

If you are thinking that Stock B is the stock with the better value since its PE is far lower than Stock A, you would be wrong.

It is true that 35 is lower than 50, but in the case of Stock B, its peer group (industry) range of PE is from a low of 16 to a high of 35.

For Stock A, its PE peer group range is from a low of 35 to a high of 166. Stock A, with a PE of 50 is near the middle of its peer group and is fairly valued.

Stock B, however, is at the high end of its peer group and, as such, is highly overvalued.

In this example, Stock A with a PE of 50 is a far better value and, therefore, much less expensive than Stock B with a PE of 35.

Looking back to our example, the two stocks were from the same industry (electric utilities), and both had identical Demand Fundamentals. By comparing the PE ratios, it becomes even more easily recognizable which one is the better value of the two.

So, to this point, when deciding between two stocks of equal or nearly equal Demand Fundamentals, consider only value from within each stock's peer group (industry). Do not consider a PE ratio without considering it from within the stock's industry range of PE ratios.

WHY SIZE MATTERS

Throughout this rule, there are some underlying assumptions: You do not have unlimited financial resources, and you cannot buy every stock you want to buy.

I am going to assume that, at this point, you have examined your personal finances enough to have made an assessment as to how much money you want to use, put at risk, or invest into the buying and selling of stock in the stock market. You should already know how many stocks you *should* own at any one time, and that number is a fixed number—meaning it doesn't fluctuate all the time.

If these two assumptions (how much money and how many stocks) are not clear in your mind, they will be by the time you finish reading the Diversification Rule and the Asset Allocation Rule later in this book.

Thus, the bottom line is that you *have* to know how much money you are going to use to build your stock portfolio. You *have* to know how many stocks you will possibly own at any one time. You must set these limits and have the discipline to stick to these limits.

Too many investors have no set strategy for buying stock. Many of them just buy a stock based on how much money they are comfortable spending at that particular time. I have seen individual investors who own stocks in over 100 different companies. They are overwhelmed with the number of different companies, and have no idea how to manage such a large group of stocks.

You may be in this position right now—too many stocks and too little time. After you read this book, you will know exactly how many stocks you need to have in your portfolio, and you will know exactly which kinds of stocks to own at any one time. Then, as you manage your world-class portfolio, you will find many situations where this Rule will help you choose between two similar stocks because you cannot own both of them.

BUILDING A BRIDGE OVER THE COLORADO RIVER AND WHY IT MATTERS TO YOUR INVESTMENT STRATEGY

In years past when we would attend the Las Vegas Money Show,[1] we would often drive over Hoover dam. We have driven over the dam many times, but the sheer size and stark landscape surrounding the beautiful Lake Mead never cease to amaze me.

---

1 The MoneyShow provides forums for stock market and financial market information.

As you may know, a bypass bridge[2] was built by the states of Nevada and Arizona and the U.S. federal government just downstream from the dam. It is was completed in 2010, and it is beautiful.

The project was a civil engineer's dream, and even though I much prefer investing in the stock market to building bridges, I must confess that every time I drive down into that canyon and drive across it on the enormous bridge structure, I am envious of the engineers who were involved in the project.

You may be wondering why I would bring the topic of building of this bridge to your attention. It is because the building of this bridge is an excellent analogy to what I am teaching you in this book.

You see, each of these rules must be considered integral building blocks to a total investment strategy and methodology. To single out one of these rules to the exclusion of the others would be like attempting to just build a highway across the Colorado River canyon below Hoover Dam without any support or structure to hold it up.

This is a great picture to illustrate my point (see Figure 1). You can see they have just completed the last of the columns that will support the highway from the foundation poured into the solid granite face of the canyon. And just below that foundation, you see the next step beginning. This is where they were slip-forming the massive arch that now extends from one side of the canyon to the other. They subsequently positioned columns between the arch and the deck of the highway above. This is truly an engineering marvel.

But, just as this structure was methodically constructed, with one careful step after another, so are we constructing an investment strategy and lifelong methodology for making consistent profits in the stock market.

---

2 The present route of U.S. 93 uses the top of Hoover Dam to cross the Colorado River. U.S. Highway 93 is the major commercial corridor between the states of Arizona, Nevada, and Utah; it is also on the North American Free Trade Agreement (NAFTA) route between Mexico and Canada. U.S. 93 was identified as a high-priority corridor in the National Highway System Designation Act of 1995. The traffic congestion caused by the inadequacy of the existing highway across the dam imposes a serious economic burden on the states of Arizona, Nevada, and Utah.

Figure 1

To bring this point home with this Rule, we have just learned why and how to properly use PE ratios as a part of your stock selection process. It would be no more right to use this rule by itself than it would to use just the part of the bridge you see in the photo. If the engineers quit at that point on the bridge, it would be useless. If they said, "Let's just concentrate on these wonderful columns and ignore the great arch that is now being built," a bridge would never span the chasm. Before anyone could drive across this bridge, all the components had to be completed and tied together in proper order and with the proper dependency one upon the other.

Just like the engineers who built this incredible, towering structure, you are now building your structure for investment success. Each Rule in this book is required and each one is dependent upon the other. Do not consider any one of these rules to be not as important as another. Just like the building of the massive arch across the canyon, that part of the bridge might be the most challenging, but the lowly piece of rebar buried in the base of one of the column foundations is no less important to the total success of the final structure. Read and study these rules with that in mind. When you complete these Rules, along with the Market-Directional Methodology Chapter, you will see how beautiful a structure you have created. But instead of something that you drive across, it will be something you can use to drive into the future as you build and grow your financial security and create wealth for you and your family.

WHAT YOU LEARNED IN THIS RULE

A lot of the work that you must do in your quest to find the right stock to buy at the right time is the work of deciding between two stocks that have nearly identical Demand Fundamentals. In this rule, you learned:

- That most investors do not have enough information or time to be a true value-type investor.
- That value, as defined by a stock's PE ratio, is a very good way to choose between two stocks of equal or nearly equal Demand Fundamentals.
- That with all other things being equal, such as the Demand Fundamentals, you should always pick the stock with the lower PE. However (and this is very important), you should only compare PEs of stocks from the same industry.

CHAPTER 4

THE TECHNICALS RULE

"If markets were efficient, traders would be extinct."

PRICING TREND + HISTORICAL VOLATILITY = MARKET TIMING SUCCESS

This rule focuses on the technical aspect of stock selection. I know you just spent the last two rules learning why fundamentals matter. Now, as we move on to why technicals matter, I want to make sure you are not confused.

In this rule, you will learn how to use pricing trends to tell you *when* to buy a stock. In the Market-Directional Methodology Chapter, you learned how and why you should not even consider buying any equity unless the market is giving you a bullish investment bias. In the Fundamentals Rule and the PE Rule, you learned how to find the stocks that you should *consider* buying, if given the go-ahead from Market-Directional Methodology Chapter. In this Rule, you will learn the first step in timing your purchase. This is the "When to Buy" rule that you will use if the market is above its Transition Zone and trending higher.

If you are new to technical analysis or have never used technicals to make trading decisions, all you have to know is that to trade like a technician, you have to learn how to read charts.

TECHNICAL ANALYSIS

Technical analysis is a method of evaluating stocks by relying on the assumption that the future share price of those stocks can be predicted by analyzing historical share price charts, historical volume charts, sector pricing charts and industry pricing charts. Technical analysis ignores fundamental analysis. The assumption is that historical charts have well-defined patterns that are highly correlated to future pricing trends. Thereby, trading decisions (buy, sell, short, or cover) can and should be made predicated on the likelihood that future pricing trends will repeat the same or similar patterns the stock exhibited in the past.

Just as there are fundamental analysts, there are also technical analysts. These two camps have a certain disdain for one another. Fundamental analysts don't believe in charting. They don't believe in the concept of reading the tea leaves of a chart to determine whether or not it is a good time to buy or sell. And technical analysts believe that fundamental analysts are out of touch with reality. They say that regardless of the fundamentals, the pricing trend could go lower or higher. Technicians want to buy on the way up and sell on the way down, regardless of the fundamentals.

I believe you have to look at *both* the fundamentals *and* the technical aspects of any stock you are about to buy or sell. You will gain insight in both approaches that significantly outweigh just using one or the other. The whole, in this case, is far more valuable than the sum of the parts.

Perhaps you already consider yourself an accomplished "technician." That is great! Some of this rule will be somewhat remedial for you, but not all of it. I use a technical approach to charting stocks that you likely will not have seen before. It is not complicated, but it utilizes the 200-day moving average with a one standard deviation of normal volatility (see the Stop Loss Rule, to learn how to calculate one standard deviation of normal volatility) 'band' on either side of the moving average. When the stock or ETF is above this band and trending higher, the equity is technically in a bullish or buy mode. When the equity is below this band and trending lower, the equity is considered to be in a bearish or sell short mode. Even if you have used technicals in your stock investment methodology for years, you should read and study this Rule. It is likely that regardless of how much you know about reading charts, trends, oscillators, patterns and triggers, you still need this Rule.

But if you have never stepped foot into the technical waters, we will cover the elementary components of technical trading so you won't be left out.

PUTTING THIS ALL IN PERSPECTIVE

I don't believe that fundamental analysis and technical analysis methodologies are mutually exclusive. Indeed, I believe that one without the other is like trying to swim with one arm while letting the other arm hang by your side. It is possible to swim with one arm, but it is very difficult. However, making stock investment decisions based on both a fundamental and a technical analysis is much like watching a champion swimmer with both arms used to propel the swimmer forward. Indeed, swimming with two arms is far more efficient and effective than just doubling the success of swimming with one arm. Likewise, using fundamentals and technicals, the stock market investor has the best chance of being more efficient and effective at generating significant and consistent profits.

With regard to technical analysis, I believe in "keeping it simple." My technical analysis methodology is simple but powerful. It is something you can actually use without spending hours and hours of studying and screening and doing what-if scenarios.

As we go through them, you will learn:

- The basic theory of technical analysis.
- How to build a simple but powerful trend line.
- How to determine what triggers a buy and what triggers a sell short, from a technical perspective.

TYPES OF TECHNICAL ANALYSIS SYSTEMS

All technical analysts have one simple objective: to determine whether a stock's price is going to move up or down in the future based on how that stock's price has moved in the past. It doesn't matter which technical system you learn or which technical charts you follow. In the end, your objective will be the same as all other technicians: you want to figure out the pricing trend of a stock. Will that trend be down so that a short trade makes sense? Or will that trend be up so that a long trade makes sense? Will the stock stop moving higher so that it can be sold at or near its top? Or will the stock stop moving lower so that it can be covered at or near its bottom?

There are many types of technical analysis systems, including:

- **Accumulation/distribution index:** A momentum indicator that tries to gauge supply and demand by discovering if investors are generally "accumulating" (buying) or "distributing" (selling) a certain stock by identifying divergences between stock price and volume flow.
- **Average true range:** A technical analysis indicator developed by J. Welles Wilder, based on trading ranges smoothed by an N-day exponential moving average (EMA).
- **Bollinger bands:** Developed by John Bollinger, Bollinger bands (lines) are plotted above and below the 21-day moving average of a stock's price. These upper and lower boundaries factor in two standard deviations (about 95 percent) of the price movement over the previous 21 days.
- **Breakout:** A chart pattern used to indicate a rise in a stock's price above its resistance level (such as its previous high price) or a drop below its support level (commonly the last lowest price).
- **The Dahl theory:** The primary theory used in this book for technical analysis wherein a stock's pricing trend is determined by how its week-ending closing price crosses a 200-day moving average of week-ending closing prices, with this trendline shifted forward in time by three weeks.

- **Hikkake pattern:** A technical analysis pattern used for determining market turning points and continuations. It is a simple pattern that can be observed in market price data, using traditional bar charts, or Japanese candlestick charts. The pattern is comprised of a measurable period of rest and volatility contraction in the market, followed by a relatively brief price move that encourages unsuspecting traders and investors to adopt a false assumption regarding the likely future direction of price.
- **Moving average convergence/divergence (MACD):** A technical analysis indicator created by Gerald Appel in the 1960s. It shows the difference between a fast and slow EMA of closing prices.
- **Momentum and rate of change:** Simple technical analysis indicators showing the difference between today's closing price and the close N days ago.
- **Money flow in technical analysis:** Typical price multiplied by volume, a kind of approximation to the dollar value of a day's trading.
- **On-balance volume:** A measure of volume distinguished as to whether trades take place on rising prices or on falling prices. Technical analysts consider great volume on rising prices bullish because it indicates the possibility that large traders are accumulating investment positions in a security.
- **Price activity (PAC) charts:** PAC charts are unique in the way they represent "volume" (the number of shares traded every day), where compound estimated volume data at each price level is plotted and color-coded.
- **Parabolic stop and reverse (SAR):** A method devised by J. Welles Wilder Jr., to find trends in market prices or securities. The concept draws on the idea that time is an enemy, and unless a security can continue to generate more profits over time, it should be liquidated.

- **Pivot point:** A means to calculate resistance and support levels, which are, in turn, used as visual cues to execute trades. Pivot point calculations provide traders with objective visual benchmarks, which some use to predict price changes.
- **Point and figure charts:** Show trends in price by, in theory, filtering out the "noise" (unimportant price movement) and focus on the main direction of the price trend and are used for longer-term price movements.
- **Relative strength index:** Developed by J. Welles Wilder, it is a financial technical analysis oscillator that shows price strength by comparing upward and downward close-to-close movements.
- **Rahul Mohindar oscillator (RMO):** A type of technical analysis developed by Rahul Mohindar of Viratech India, which detects trends in financial markets and is designed to work on open-high-low-close charts.
- **Stochastic oscillator:** A momentum indicator, introduced by George Lane in the 1950s, to compare the closing price of a commodity to its price range over a given time span.
- **Trix oscillator:** Shows the slope (i.e., derivative) of a triple-smoothed exponential moving average. The name trix is from "triple exponential." It was developed in the 1980s by Jack Hutson, editor of Technical Analysis of Stocks and Commodities magazine.
- **Williams %R oscillator:** Developed by Larry Williams, it is a technical analysis oscillator that shows the current closing price in relation to the high and low of the past N days (for a given N).

Some of these strategies are better than others. A lot of the value in any of these approaches has a lot to do with the proficiency you develop in using them and the discipline that you use in the implementation of these strategies.

READING CHARTS IS EASY—FINDING THE RIGHT CHART TO READ IS THE KEY

Don't be daunted by the idea of learning to read charts. If you have never attempted to follow or even understand the concept of technical analysis, reading and studying this rule will turn you into an excellent stock technician.

Figure 4.1 shows a simple technical chart of AAPL (Apple, Inc.).

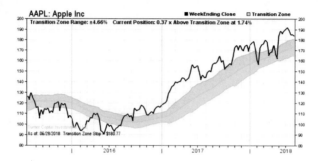

Figure 4.1

This is an easy chart to read, and as we move further into thebook, the charts don't get much more complicated.

The black line is the week-ending closing price of AAPL over a 3-year timeframe. The yellow band is the 200-day moving average plus/minus one standard deviation of normal volatility of the stock, based on the prior 12 months, as expected for the upcoming 5 trading days. I call this band, the "Transition Zone" because the equity is transitioning from bullish to bearish or bearish to bullish. When the stock's price is inside the Transition Zone, it is one of the highest risk periods of time to own a stock or ETF. I make it a rule to sell any position that moves from above to inside the Transition Zone; and to cover any short position that moves from below to inside the Transition Zone.

This moving average is based on the average of the 40 most recent week-ending closing prices of a stock.

200-day Moving Average Trend Line

A 200-day moving average is simply the average of 40 week-ending closing prices, which is updated weekly by dropping the oldest value (41 weeks ago) and then adding the newest value (this week's week-ending closing price) and recalculating the average. A 200-day moving average of stock would be calculated by summing the last 40 week-ending closing prices and then dividing that total by 40. Each week, you would drop the oldest week-ending closing price and calculate the average with the most recent 40 week-ending closing prices in its place. Then, you take that average and plot it on the chart for that particular week. The width of the band around the 200-day moving average varies based on the recorded volatility of the prior 12 months pricing action of the equity.

From this chart, you have all the timing information you need to make a trading decision; keeping in mind that you should not even consider buying any equity unless the market is above its Transition Zone and trending higher. Here is how it works:

- When the week-ending price (black line) crosses from inside the Transition Zone (yellow band) to above the band, the equity is considered to have entered a bullish condition and is a candidate to buy.
- When the week-ending price crosses from above to inside the Transition Zone, the equity is considered to have moved from being in a bullish trend, but has not yet signaled that it is in a bearish trend. It is, rather, "transitioning" from bullish to either bearish or back to being bullish. In either case, since a well-defined trend has not yet developed, the objective would be to not own the equity when it is inside the Transition (yellow) band.
- When the week-ending price crosses from inside the Transition Zone to below the band, the equity is considered to be in a bearish trend. When an equity is below the Transition Zone AND trending lower, a short or inverse investment strategy is worth consideration.

There are many nuances to technical charts, and we will get into some of the more important nuances throughout the rest of the book. But, the concept is no more complicated than this: You determine when to buy and when to sell short by watching how the price of a stock moves above or below the stock's Transition Zone.

When the stock's price moves above the Transition Zone, the technical odds favor buying.

When the stock's price moves below the Transition Zone, the technical odds favor selling short.

It doesn't get a lot more complicated than that. But there is one thing that I must hasten to add at this point:

You don't have enough information to start buying and shorting yet. You must put all the rules into your investment methodology before jumping into the market and especially the information contained in Chapter 1, The Market-Directional Methodology Chapter. It would be a big mistake for you to chart a few stocks, slap on a trend line, and start buying and shorting. Please wait until you have finished this book before putting any of these rules to work.

BUILDING THE RIGHT TECHNICAL CHART

I use stock charts to tell me when to get in the market (buy or short), but I use what I call my "Intelligent Stop Loss®" formula, which is registered with the U.S. Patent Office, to tell me when to get out. You will learn all about the Intelligent Stop Loss® formula in the Stop Loss Rule.

The objective of all technical analysis is to determine the best time to buy and the best time to sell an equity in order to achieve the highest return for the least risk.

Every investor wants to buy stocks that are trending higher in market price, and for stocks that are trending lower in market price investors will either sell their long positions or sell short.

It doesn't matter what technical system you use; your goal will be to know the difference between normal volatility and a change in the overall direction of the stock's market price. Why? Because if a stock's price moves lower due to normal volatility, but is still trending higher, you typically want to hold onto the position. However, if a stock's price moves against you by more than its normal volatility, the odds favor the fact that the downward move is not just normal volatility, but is a change in trend and signals it is a time to exit the trade.

Remember: Never buy a stock unless it is supported by both technical and fundamental buy signals.

As I mentioned earlier, you can use any technical system you want, but you must use one. A little earlier in this rule, you learned how to read a very simple chart of AAPL. You learned about a moving average and a volatility band; and what to do when a stock's price moved above or below that band.

Take a look at the chart in Figure 4.2. This is an expanded set of charts all pertaining to AAPL.

You will notice that the main (upper) chart is a three-year chart of Apple just like the chart you saw in Figure 4.1. There is a lot of information in Figure 4.2 including:

- Main chart (the stock pricing chart)
- On this chart, you can see the week-ending market price of AAPL, including the 200-day moving average (trend line) and associated Transition Zone. This chart gives you an easy-to-read indication of whether you should own the stock, have a short position in the stock, or have no position in the stock at all. As you learned earlier in this rule, depending on whether the stock's week-ending price is above the Transition Zone or below it, you will immediately know if you should have any position in the stock. If the week-ending share price is sufficiently above the Transition Zone, it is okay to own the stock. If the week-ending share price is sufficiently below the Transition Zone, it is okay to short the stock. If the week-ending share price is inside the yellow band, then you should not be long or short the stock.

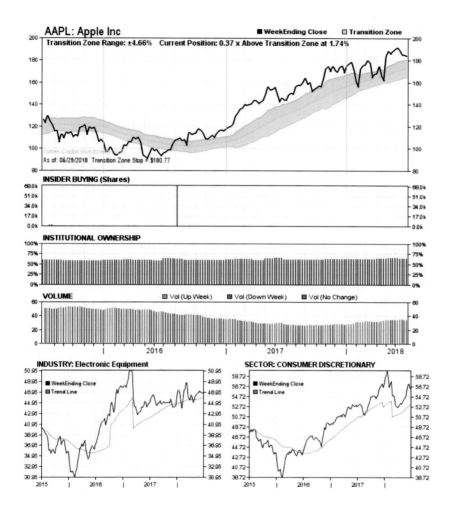

Figure 4.2—Expanded AAPL

LONG POSITION

A long position means that you have purchased the stock with the expectation that its market price will increase over time. Unlike shorting a stock, the most you can lose is your entire investment if the price of the stock goes to zero.

SHORT POSITION

A short position means that, through your broker, you borrow shares of the stock and immediately sell those shares where you are paid by the buyer. Your assumption is that the market price of the shares will decrease over time. At some point in the future, hopefully, when the market price of the stock is lower, you buy the same number of shares you borrowed earlier and give them back to your broker. You get to keep the difference between the price at which you sold the shares immediately after you borrowed them, less the amount you paid to buy them back. Of course, if the stock's market price moved higher after you borrowed the shares and sold them, you would have to buy the shares back at a higher price to return the shares to the broker. In a short sale, it is possible to lose more than your total investment.

SPLITS

When a company decides that it wants to have more shares of its stock available to the public, but at a lower price, and it does not want to issue new shares, the company will execute a corporate action in which all of its outstanding shares are divided into multiple shares. For example, if a company splits its stocks 2-for-1, it means that for every share currently traded on the open market, those shares immediately double in number, while at the same time, the price per share is reduced by 50 percent. Although the number of outstanding shares doubled, the total dollar value of the shares remains the same compared to presplit market price. This is because no real value was added as a result of the split.

INSIDER BUYING

You will learn more about insider buying in the Insider Buying Rule.

This part of the chart indicates whether insiders are buying or not. I don't care about insider selling, as that can happen for lots of reasons other than the insider not liking the stock; but, nothing and no one forces an insider to buy. When an insider buys, it can only be for one reason: They believe their money will grow faster with their own stock than in any other investment.

WEEKLY TRADING VOLUME

Watching the total trading volume of a stock can tell you a lot of information about the strength or weakness of the stock's market pricing trend. I prefer to own stocks with plenty of liquidity, so the higher the average daily volume, the better.The green vertical bars are "up volume," which tells you that the stock's market price is increasing as the trade volume of shares increases. You can infer from this action that the market likes this stock and it is likely that more investors are buying more shares. At the very least, you know that more shares are being traded at increasing market prices.

- The red vertical bars are "down volume," which tells you that the stock's market price is decreasing as the trade volume of shares decreases. You can infer from this action that the market is not as enamored with the stock at that time, as more investors are selling more shares. At the very least, you know that more shares are being traded as the stock's market price is decreasing.

INDUSTRY CHART

There is no better gauge of how strong a stock's pricing trend is, than by knowing how a particular stock's "market" is moving. The two best indicators of how bullish or bearish the market is, with regard to a specific stock, are its industry and sector (more on sector later). The industry chart is a chart of the average market price of every stock in a particular stock's industry. In this case, with AAPL, the industry is "personal computers." This industry chart includes:

- A 200-day moving average trend line, which displays the average week-ending closing price of all the stocks in the stock's industry.
- If the average price of every stock in the industry is above the trend line, the industry is considered in "bull mode." This means that more money is flowing into this industry than out of it. It means that more investors have a positive opinion of this industry than a negative opinion.

In a "rising-tide-lifts-all-boats" environment, a stock that has strong Demand Fundamentals and is in a technical buy mode, and has its industry and sector in bull mode, you should draw the conclusion that there is a lot of pressure on your stock's market price to move higher. This is the exact scenario that you must look for in your technical analysis.

Sector chart

Although I put more emphasis on a stock's industry bull or bear mode condition, certainly it is a major positive when both the stock's industry and sector are bull mode. In Figure 4.2, you can see AAPL's sector chart. The sector chart is a chart of the average market price of every stock in the stock's sector. In this case, AAPL's sector is "technology." This sector chart includes:

- A 200-day moving average trend line, which charts the average week-ending closing price of all the stocks in the stock's sector.
- If the average price of every stock in the sector is above the trend line, the sector is considered in "bull mode." This means that more money is flowing into this sector than out of it. It means that more investors have a positive opinion of this sector.

By looking at Figure 4.3, you get information telling you when to get into a stock for either a long or a short trade. You also can use this chart to help you determine your exit strategy (more on this later).

When a stock's week-ending closing price moves above the Transition Zone, the stock has given a technical buy signal. When the week-ending closing price moves below the Transition Zone, the stock has given a technical short sell signal.

I use a stop loss strategy (The Intelligent Stop Loss® strategy, which will be covered in the Stop Loss Rule) to tell me when to sell a long

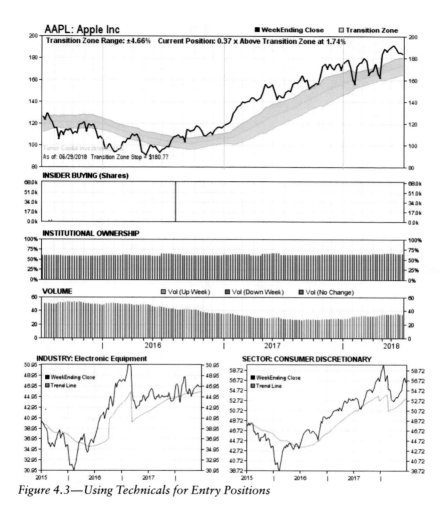

Figure 4.3—Using Technicals for Entry Positions

position or cover a short position. When a stock triggers its stop loss setting, the pricing trend of the stock has moved from normal volatility to a change in direction of the pricing trend of the stock. When a stock's pricing trend reverses, as indicated by triggering a stop, it is time to exit the trade.

I realize all of this can be a bit overwhelming, especially since these charts cannot be easily reproduced without a program designed and written specifically for this technical strategy. However, you can access to these charts at www.TurnerTrends.com. While there is a nominal subscription price, you get a 30-day money-back guarantee, so you can see all that I am showing you in this book for 30 days for free to see what I am talking about. But, you can get very close to this same concept by using a standard 200-day moving average and Bollinger bands set at a 200-day time period and utilizing one standard deviation.

So, the actual concept is very simple:

- You execute a buy when the week-ending price of the stock crosses from inside to above the Transition Zone.
- You execute a sell short when the week-ending price of the stock crosses from inside to below the Transition Zone.
- You sell long positions or short positions when the stock's price reaches the stop loss price.

Allow me to summarize to this point. In Chapter 2, The Fundamentals Rule, you learned how to pick the stocks that you would consider buying if the timing was right. In Chapter 3, The PE Rule, you learned how to spend your money wisely when buying a stock. And here, in Chapter 4, The Technicals Rule, you are learning how to know when it is the right time to buy one of the stocks that meets the fundamentals criteria. Bottom -line: you should consider buying a stock only if it has strong Demand Fundamentals and its price has moved above the Transition Zone.

AVOID THE NOISE OF THE MARKET

As you develop your trading and investment strategy, you have to make very singular decisions (buy, sell, sell short, cover) from a plethora of inputs. These rules provide you with an easy-to-follow road map that simply and effectively navigates your decision-making process through a maze of data to a decision that you can believe in and that will give you confidence in your stock selections.

As investors, we are inundated with information. The vast amount of information spewing from the Internet, TV, radio, newspapers, analysts, company financial reports, and the like is indeed mind-boggling. Buried within that mountain of data is the knowledge that we seek. The knowledge that we want is: what to buy; when to buy, and, most importantly, when to sell.

If you master these rules, you will learn how to emotionally distance yourself from the minute-by-minute, hour-by-hour, or day-by-day vagaries of the market. You will learn how to rapidly turn overwhelming amounts of information into a few wonderful and critically important nuggets of knowledge.

For example: If the market is up 200 points on Monday and down 300 points on Tuesday, then back up 50 points on Wednesday, such whipsaws and volatility in the market can overwhelm your emotions. One day, you think you should be in the market; the next day, you think you should be out, only to reverse that thinking again the following day.

I consider the cacophony of information and the volatility of the market during the week as just so much "noise." Making investment decisions in the din of so much market noise invariably leads to mistakes.

A far better approach is to let the markets close for the week, gather your data, and then, in the relative peace and quiet of the weekend when the market sleeps a couple of days, take a deep breath and make your trading decisions. Look at the week's market activity from the perspective of the weekend.

When determining trends, it is extremely important to remove noise from your decision making. Noise can drown out important considerations. Noise can be the news, analyst upgrades and downgrades, talking heads on TV, geopolitical events, and a host of other distracting information. Noise can also be a part of your data, in the form of outliers and volatility. It is important to reduce and/or eliminate as much noise from your analysis as possible.

It doesn't matter that much what happened day to day; what really matters is how each stock's price changed from end of week to end of week.

I want you to get away from watching too much stock market news. Turn the TV off. Follow these rules and then spend more time doing things other than worrying about buying and selling stocks.

In these rules, you are going to learn how to build a world-class stock portfolio and make all your trades and set all the upcoming week's exit strategies in a couple of hours on the weekend. The rest of your life should be devoted to more important activities than the stock market.

Think of yourself as a long-term investor, one week at a time!

READING THE TEA LEAVES

Depending on the technical system that you follow, reading and understanding technical charts can be more than a bit difficult. You saw that long list of methodologies espoused by different theorists, and that is a list of only the most recognized ones. Frankly, I have never seen a complex technical system provide any significant increase in net total return over what you get from simple technical methodologies. In fact, I have seen just the opposite. Often, the simpler the technical approach, the more easily you can detect strong trading signals. The better the trading signals, the more profit you will move to the bottom line.

Now, let's move back to the chart in Figure 4.2 on AAPL. I want you to pay close attention to the far right side of the main (top) chart.

You see how the stock's price dropped suddenly in January of 2018. The stock triggered its stop in late January; moved well down into its Transition Zone and nearly broke through into a bearish condition before it recovered and moved back above the Transition Zone, where it gave a new buy signal.

You might say that there was no sense in selling in January and then buying back in February, but, actually, there was a LOT of sense in the trades. First of all, you never know when the market is going to correct by 20%, 30%, 40% or more, moving well into bear territory. When you got out of AAPL in late January, you took the risk of an extended bear market correction completely off the table for AAPL. The fact that the sell-off was short-lived is not the point. The point is you didn't lose any money in getting out and then back in at almost the same price, but in the meantime you took enormous risk of loss out of the equation. The methodology worked to perfection.

You want to be in the market and growing capital when risk is lower, but you want to be in cash and safely on the sidelines when risk is higher.

OUTLIER

An outlier is a number in a set of data that is much larger or smaller than most of the other numbers in the set. With regard to the Rules in this book, all trends are based on week-ending closing share prices. Other than the impact to stop loss settings and/or stop loss orders, intraweek share prices are irrelevant. Likewise, intraweek market movement is irrelevant. The only data used for trend analysis is based on the week-ending closing prices for stocks and/or markets. Wild changes in prices during the week are considered to be irrelevant and not to be included in the development of trend lines. These atypical stock or market prices are considered as outliers and are ignored.

The point to all of this is that these are profoundly powerful charts that can give you an excellent indication of when to buy and when to short. Of course, you want to buy only fundamentally strong stocks, but the timing of your buying and selling is how you make consistently significant profits in the stock market! I know it works. I've done it. And you can, too!

CALCULATING THE ANNUALIZED RETURN

To calculate the annualized return, divide the time the investment is held into the total number of trading days in the year, which is about 255 trading days. Then multiply that number by the net return. The assumption is that you could make the same amount the rest of the year that you did in the shorter time period.

WHAT YOU LEARNED IN THIS RULE

This is the rule that tells you when to buy. You learned:

- That it is good to own fundamentally strong stocks that have upward pricing trends.
- That reading and understanding technical stock charts will provide the knowledge of which direction a stock's price is most likely to move.
- Why it is important to remove market and data noise from your decision-making process.
- How to build and read a technical stock chart.
- How to recognize when a stock triggers a buy signal and when it triggers a short sell signal.

CHAPTER 5

THE STOP LOSS RULE

"The best stress reliever is a smart stop loss order!"

UNREALIZED GAIN + STOP LOSS ORDER = LESS STRESS AND MORE CONSISTENT PROFITS

So far you've learned the principles of Demand Fundamentals, the use of the price-to-earnings (PE) ratio to avoid buying expensive stocks, and the basis of technical analysis for picking the right time to open a new trade. In this rule, you will learn the *right time to exit* a position. This rule is called the "Intelligent Stop Loss®" rule.

Next to the Market-Directional Methodology Chapter, I believe this is one of the single most important concepts in my book. There should be a huge star beside this Rule! I have been "saved" from many whipsaw sessions in the market by using this strategy.

WHIPSAW

Whipsaw is when a stock's market price makes a quick move up or down, followed by a sharp price change in the opposite direction. All too often, an investor will buy or short on a whipsaw event, only to be fooled by the sudden reversal and have to either sell or cover. Generally, an investor gets whipsawed when he or she does not follow a rigid set of rules that governs the timing of entry and exit points.

The objective of this rule is to hold onto a stock as long as it is making you money. "Making you money" is the important phrase here. It means you want to hold onto a stock as long as the stock's market price is trending or moving in the direction that provides an increasing level of unrealized gain.

Unrealized gain is the profit you would make, in terms of real dollars, if you were to sell a stock at the current market price, if the current market price is more than you originally paid for the stock. Conversely, "unrealized loss" is the actual dollar amount you would lose if you were to sell the stock at the current market price, where the current market price of the stock is less than the amount you originally paid for the stock. With regard to short selling, unrealized gain is the difference between the amount of the stock when you borrowed and then sold the shares, compared to the current market price of the stock if you were to buy the same number of shares and return those shares to your broker, assuming the current market price of the stock is less than the price you sold them for when you initiated the trade. Conversely, in a short sale, if the price of the stock has moved higher from the price at which you sold the shares when you put on the trade, the difference would be your unrealized loss.

The term *unrealized* means that until you close the trade—meaning until such time as you sell a long position or cover a short position—you have not actually made or lost any money, regardless of the difference between the price of your stock when you initiated the trade and just prior to your closing the trade. An unrealized profit becomes a real profit when you close out a trade and convert your shares back to cash. The same is true for an unrealized loss. The loss does not become "real" until you close out of your position in the shares originally bought or sold short.

A good approach is to maintain two sets of running totals on your portfolio. One is based on the total value of your portfolio (including cash and equities) at the beginning of each year or month or inception and the current value of your portfolio (including cash and equities). This would give you the total profit or loss, including all unrealized gains and losses. The other is based purely on net cash gain or loss. In this approach, you assume the beginning value was zero and you track only the net result of closed trades. If a closing trade results in a net cash loss, your net cash profit moves lower. If a closing trade results in a net cash gain, your net cash profit moves higher.

Both of these views of your investment strategy are important. The best way to measure real performance of your stock market trading prowess is to monitor your net cash gain or loss. All unrealized gains and losses can change in a moment, depending on the vagaries of the market.

Now that you've read this rather lengthy explanation, let me summarize our main objective: If you are long in a position, you want the stock's pricing trend or directional movement, to be higher and higher. You want just the opposite if you are short in a position. The key to making consistent profits in the stock market is to only keep stocks in your portfolio that are making you more and more money and get out of those that are not making you money.

GOING WITH THE FLOW

I believe there is an ideal place or position to maintain when you are riding in an up-and-down market (which is pretty much the kind of market we have all the time). I often use the following story to illustrate why it is important to not get out of sync with the market.

I want you to pretend that you are a wildebeest roaming the great African savanna. You are not by yourself. In fact, you are mingling with a great herd of wildebeests. You have only one enemy in life: the lions.

The herd starts moving across the savanna. It just so happens to be moving from the lower left to the upper right. This makes you very happy. You are happiest when the herd is moving from the lower left to the upper right and you are the saddest when the herd moves from the upper left to the lower right.

But, at the moment, life is good. You are with the herd, and the herd is moving in the right direction. Now, let me ask you a question: Just where in the herd are you? Are you out at the edges of the herd or are you right in the middle?

If you are a smart wildebeest—and I am sure you are way above average—then you are not out at the edge of the herd. Why do I think that? Because I am sure you already know what happens to you if you hang around at the edge of the herd. The lions can pick you off!! Those at the edge of the herd are always fearful and are never too sure when the herd will suddenly veer one way or the other and leave them alone and stranded in the midst of lion country.

You, of course, know of these things and you are smart to stay as close to the middle of the herd as you can.

Now, let's move this story from the world of imagination to the real world of stock market investing. As a stock market investor, you want to move with the herd.

I know, you've been told that to make money in the market, you *must* think outside the box, you must be a maverick, you must *not* have a "herd" mentality—you *must not* go with the herd.

I suspect that the *only* reason you have ever been told that is the person doing the talking has no idea how to follow the herd and how to make money by following the herd. In fact, that person has no idea how to take advantage of market movements, so they try to justify their complete lack of being able to capitalize on market movements by saying you shouldn't follow the market.

I tell you it is imperative that you learn how to follow the market. It is the *only* way to consistently make superior profits and maintain significantly low risk. I know how exciting it is to be a maverick and run outside the herd. But, if you want to be a maverick and run around outside the herd, you had better be fast and tough. The lions, which in this case would be a sudden reversal in your stock's pricing trend, are anxiously waiting for you.

It is far better to be safe and secure by staying in the middle of the herd and to own stocks that are moving higher because that is the direction the herd is moving than to be outside the herd where the risk is high and results can be financially life threatening.

I believe in low risk, but I also believe in getting the best returns I can without incurring too much risk. The investment strategy contained within these rules will achieve that objective.

Remember, when your stocks are moving in price from the lower left of the chart to the upper right, you want to be in the middle of the herd. There is no sense in your trying to find a stock that the market has little, if any, interest in and does not have a herd of investors pushing its price higher and higher. No, your job is to find those high-quality stocks that the whole herd ("market") likes and buy in early, then ride merrily along with the market as long as your stock's price is moving higher.

But, unlike the wildebeest, which must stay with the herd or be eaten by the lions, when the herd suddenly veers away from pushing your stock from the lower left to the upper right, you can simply sell your shares for a profit and look for another opportunity where the herd has picked up another high-quality stock and is once again pushing it from lower left to upper right.

The key, of course, is to know when your stock has reached its upward pricing trend and is about to start moving lower. All stocks cycle through times of upward pricing trends and lowering pricing trends. No equity's pricing trend moves in a straight line. Some of that movement is just normal volatility. Some of that movement is directional, where the general pricing trend of the equity is moving either lower, higher, or sideways. Every investor wants to know the difference between normal volatility and a change in pricing trend.

Investors would be far wealthier if they could distinguish the difference between normal volatility and a complete change in direction of the pricing trend of a stock. As you learned in the Technicals Rule, every technical system ever created or that ever will be created has this as its primary objective—to know the difference between volatility and a change in direction of the pricing trend of a stock.

Sideways

When a stock trades "sideways," it means that the stock is trading in a very narrow range over an extended period of time.

To make a profit, you must first buy a stock and then sell it later at a higher price, of course. Traveling with the herd can help you do this, while at the same time lower your risk. But, surprisingly, many investors do not consciously know the primary reason why they buy stocks. You should know one very important—might I say, critically important—aspect of stock market investing. You **must** know the **primary** reason to **own a stock**. Without this knowledge, there is no sense in your buying one more share of stock.

The Primary Reason to Own Stocks

You never make money by *buying* the right stock at the right time; you can make money only by *selling* the right stock at the right time.

Let me repeat that, "You *never* make money in the stock market by buying the right stock at the right time—never. You will make money in the stock market *only* by selling the right stock at the right time—and, of course, at the right price!"

How many times have you heard someone say, "If only I had bought that stock at the right time, I would be rich by now" or "It seems like I always buy the really good stocks at the wrong time"?

Stock market investors are, typically, obsessed with buying the right stock at the right time. They seem to think that is all that matters. They read financial journals. They go to investor conferences. They attend local chapters of investment groups. They listen to the talking heads on the financial news channels. They subscribe to investment newsletters. They do this for one reason and one reason only: They want to find the next stock to buy. They are obsessed with and singularly focused on buying the right stock at the right time. They do this because they think that the most important part of stock market investing is to buy the right stock at the right time because they think that is how they will make a profit and grow their portfolio. *They could not be further from the truth!*

Buying the right stock at the right time only exchanges your cash for shares of equal value. Nothing has changed except that you had cash and now you have shares. You haven't made a dime or lost a dime; you have only exchanged one asset for another of equal value—dollars for shares.

Stock market investors generally spend a lot of time thinking about *what* to buy. Most investors will research companies before buying stock in those companies. They will go through no small amount of fundamental and technical analysis to make their final decision on what to buy. This is a good thing, although they often spend too much time researching the wrong data (review the Fundamentals Rule).

Once they have bought a stock, they believe the hard part is done, but it isn't. These investors sit back and wait for their wonderful stock picks to climb higher and higher. Sometimes, their stocks do move higher and higher; other times, those stocks tend to move lower and lower. Still other times, they move sideways—up for a while and down for a while.

The single most important thing you can do as a stock market investor is to sell your stocks at the right time. In fact, **the number one reason for buying a stock is to sell that stock and sell it at a profit.** Why? Because you never actually make a dime out of a trade until you sell. Anything else is just a paper profit or a paper loss. Holding a stock with unrealized gains does avoid having to pay taxes on the gains, but the problem is that those unrealized gains can turn into realized losses if you do not sell at the right time. Bernard Baruch is often quoted as saying his biggest fault with his investing strategy was that he "always sold too soon."

You can't do much with unrealized gains or losses. You can't spend unrealized gains. You can't buy a new house with unrealized gains. You can't buy food or pay for college with unrealized gains. Sure, you might be able to borrow money against unrealized gains, but that is extremely risky. Remember, the key to making consistent profits in the stock market is to consistently turn unrealized gains into realized gains. That event occurs only when you *sell at a profit.*

BERNARD BARUCH

Bernard Baruch was born in Camden, South Carolina, to Simon and Belle Baruch. He was the second of four sons. His father, Simon, was a German immigrant of Jewish ethnicity who came to the United States in 1855. He became a surgeon on the staff of Confederate General Robert E. Lee during the American Civil War. In 1881 the family moved to New York City, and Bernard Baruch graduated from the City College of New York eight years later. He eventually became a broker and then a partner in the firm of A. Housman and Company. With his earnings and commissions he bought a seat on the New York Stock Exchange for $18,000 (approximately $458,000 in 2007 dollars). There, he amassed a fortune before the age of 30 via speculation in the sugar market. In 1903 he had his own brokerage firm and had gained the reputation of "The Lone Wolf on Wall Street" because of his refusal to join any other financial house. By 1910, he had become one of Wall Street's financial leaders.

However, most investors will tell you that they either have no idea when to sell or that selling is the single most difficult decision they try to make. There is almost always a lot of second-guessing and what-if'ing going on when an investor is trying to decide whether to sell some or all of a stock.

So, what can you do when a stock you own moves against you? Do you always know if it is better to sell or to hold on a little longer? After you finish this rule, you will *always* know exactly what to do after you have bought a stock. You will *always* know exactly when to sell.

BUT WHEN SHOULD I SELL?

Each year, I speak to literally thousands of stock market investors. These investors come in all varieties. Some are seasoned investors, some are buy-and-hold investors, some just own mutual funds, some are day traders, some are momentum traders, some are just getting started. Some have millions of dollars in the stock market; some have only a few thousand. But, invariably, most of them all have the same common problem— they have no idea when to sell.

Learn this rule and you will *always* know when to sell. You see, knowing when to sell is a formula. It's not guesswork, and it's not closing your eyes and grimacing while saying to yourself, "I hope I'm doing the right thing, selling this one!" You do not have to rely on emotion or gut feeling. When you come to realize that your number one reason for buying a stock is to sell it and start using the formula in this rule to determine the sell price, you will become a far, far wealthier investor.

In fact, if I've helped you realize already that the only reason to buy a stock is to sell it, then you are more than halfway to mastering this rule. But most investors never know for sure when it is time to sell. They ask themselves:

- Have I made enough profit?
- Should I sell before this week's earnings report?
- I'm losing money on this stock, but should I hold onto it a while longer and see if it goes back up?
- I've lost so much on this stock, how can I sell now and lose so much of my investment?
- Analysts say the price target on this stock is much higher than it is now. Should I hold on?
- I bought this stock based on its strong fundamentals. The fundamentals haven't changed, but the stock is down 20 percent from where I bought it. Should I hold on? Should I buy more and average down my net basis?
- I really like what this company does. I don't understand why the stock's price keeps dropping. Should I sell now or wait for the market to turn around?
- I can't believe I am in the same predicament again. I bought this stock at the top and now have lost so much. I know that just as soon as I sell it, the stock will rebound. What can I do to get out of this horrible and expensive vicious cycle? It happens to me every time.

Of course, before you sell a stock, you must first buy it. Most investors would use one or more of the following reasons to buy a stock:

- The stock has great fundamentals.
- The stock has perfect technicals.
- The stock has been highly recommended by very knowledgeable investors.
- The stock has an incredible dividend.
- The stock has the number one rating in the current *Investor's Business Daily* 100 Top-Rated Stocks (IBD-100).
- Your broker said this stock is a "lock."
- It is the best stock to own according to all 10 of the rules in this book!

Yet, none of the above constitutes the ***primary*** *reason to buy* a stock. Some of these reasons are valid for picking the best stock to buy, but none of these reasons are why you should buy any stock.

Think about this: At the very beginning of this book, I listed many reasons why people invest in the stock market. Regardless of those reasons, each reason has one real objective: *to make a reasonably high rate of return on capital at an acceptable level of risk.*

To make money in the stock market, there are only two critical steps you must take:

1. Buy shares.
2. Sell those shares at a profit.

This is a simple credo, but it is extremely important. I want you to commit these next few words to memory and make them a part of your investment DNA:

The *only reason* to buy a stock is to *sell it!*

After reading this rule and applying this rule to your current investing strategy, you will *never* worry about when to sell again—*ever!*

INVESTMENT DNA

DNA is the material inside the nucleus of cells that carries the genetic blueprint of life. In this case, "investment DNA" is the blueprint of how an individual invests in the stock market.

TIMING IS EVERYTHING

This strategy will achieve two very important goals for you:

1. Mitigate downside risk.
2. Provide you with the <u>right</u> price and the <u>right</u> time to sell.

If the primary reason to buy a stock is to sell it, it naturally follows that you need to know the timing and the price for selling. Not every stock you buy is going to move higher in price. Even if you follow 100 percent of the rules in this book, some of your stock picks will be losers. An extremely important part of making consistent profits in the stock market is to know when to get out of losing positions.

Let's assume you have just selected a stock for several reasons, one of which is the stock's pricing trend is moving higher and you want to take advantage of that trend. You buy the stock and then it begins to move lower and lower, reversing its uptrend to a downtrend. What do you do? First of all, how do you even know if the trend has reversed? How do you know it is not just a normal downtick in volatility?

If a stock's price drops due to normal volatility, it will soon recover and continue to move upward. However, when a stock's pricing trend reverses, it can show a very similar price drop as it moves against you.

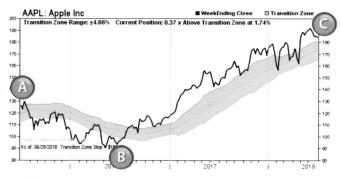

Figure 5.1

Take a look at Figure 5.1. This is a chart of Apple, Inc. over about a three-year period between 2015 and 2018.

As you can see, AAPL had a spectacular rise from Circle B to Circle C, as its price moved from about $90 to $180. And, to be clear, you would have made money even if you had bought at Circle A and held on all the way down to the bottom and then back up to Circle C. But, consider how you had to go through a 31% loss from Circle A to Circle B. And, it took you nearly a year after the bottom at Circle B just to get back to even. Wouldn't it have been far better to have sold your shares at Circle A and then bought back in after the shares bottomed at Circle B? Of course, you learned in the Market-Directional Methodology Chapter, there is a right time and a wrong time to be buying. Mastering that Chapter will help you make these kinds of trades routinely and safely without guessing about tops or bottoms.

You want to own a stock only as long as its pricing trend is moving with you and you want to sell the stock when its pricing trend reverses direction and moves against you. But, no stock only moves in a straight direction. Every stock vacillates up and down over time. This vacillation is called, "volatility". Volatility is not the same thing as "trend".

MOVES AGAINST YOU

"Moves against you" means that the price of the stock moves in the opposite direction of your objective. For long positions, the stock's price moves lower. For short positions, the stock's price moves higher. In either case, the stock's pricing trend is moving against you.

As long as a stock is trending higher (assuming you are long the position), you want to own it. *But,* and this is important, as soon as you can detect that a stock's pricing trend has reversed direction, you want to get out of the position, take your profits and look for a better equity to own. So, the key to making the right decision regarding when to sell, is to know (measure) the difference between the stock's pricing moving against you due to normal volatility and a change in trend. If the move against you is merely normal volatility, you will want to stay in the trade. If, on the other hand, the move against you is a trend reversal where the stock has moved (past tense is important to grasp here), you will want to sell and exit the trade.

Referring back to Figure 5.1... At Circle A, when the stock moved into the yellow band (Transition Zone), the proper course of action was to sell and go to cash. If you are comfortable with shorting, you could consider shorting AAPL when it moved below the Transition Zone (about 3 months following Circle A). Regardless, you would not want to buy AAPL stock again until it reverses trend at Circle B and moves up, through and exits above the Transition Zone, about 2 months following the bottom at Circle B. Why wait so long to get back in? The answer is simple: Until the price moves back up above the Transition Zone, there is too much risk of a trend reversal.

The quickest way to lose money in the stock market is to take on too much risk at the wrong time.

My point is this: Measuring and not guessing are everything when it comes to making money in the stock market. And the best way to measure your entry and exit points is through the use of a technical system that tells you when to buy and when to sell.

THE INTELLIGENT STOP LOSS® STRATEGY

To avoid getting trapped into a stock that is falling in price you should always have a predetermined sell price—*always!*

To accomplish this task, I strongly recommend using a stop loss strategy. You need a stop loss order that meets the following criteria:

- The price at which you can be relatively certain that the stock has reversed direction and is moving lower.
- The maximum amount of loss you are willing to accept and not be outside your loss comfort zone.
- The price you are willing to take for your stock after you have made a profit.

All stocks move up and down during a trading week. This movement is normal and considered nothing more than volatility. The key is to know the difference between normal volatility and when to exit a trade. To know this, you must be able to differentiate between normal volatility and a change in the directional pricing trend of the stock.

As I have said many times, the objective of every technical system, regardless of its methodology, is to know the difference between volatility and a change in trend. The Intelligent Stop Loss® strategy provides that critical piece of knowledge. The formula is predicated on the following assumptions:

Stop Loss Order

A stop loss order is an order to close out the trade (sell if long or cover if short) if and when the stock touches or moves through the stop loss order price.

Loss Comfort Zone

"Loss comfort zone" is the percentage of loss you can experience on a single trade and not lose sleep at night. Every investor has a loss comfort zone, beyond which they will become very fearful and uncomfortable. If you invest in the stock market, you are guaranteed to lose money on some trades. This will be true even if you follow each of the rules in this book explicitly. Some investors can tolerate a loss of 20 percent on a single trade; some 10 percent; some as much as 50 percent or more; and some as little as 5 percent. Only you know your own loss comfort zone and your tolerance for loss.

- Stop loss orders are to be set one week at a time.
- The data used in the formula are based on the most recent trading week and the most recent trading year.
- Historical volatility will not appreciably change in the upcoming 5 trading days when compared to previous 52 weeks of historical volatility.
- If a stock's market price moves below the calculated stop loss price, that stock's pricing trend has reversed from moving higher to moving lower.
- If a stock's market price moves above the calculated stop loss price, for short positions, the stock's pricing trend has reversed from moving lower to moving higher.

This stop loss formula has been tested and back tested in thousands of real-world trading situations. It has been tested on both stocks and exchange-traded funds (ETFs) and in markets spanning more than 50 years. Will it give you the perfect stop loss setting every single time? *No.* But will it make you a wealthier investor and lower your risk in the market at the same time? *Yes.*

Remember, the stock market is a very dynamic and often imperfect process where buyers and sellers are often swayed as much or more by emotion than fact. Inconsistencies, surprises, breaking news, geopolitical and economic eruptions abound, and always will. Data are often lagging indicators, and trends become more difficult to predict. But trends do develop, and the investor who ignores these trends is likely to be the poorer for it.

The objective of my stop loss formula is to provide the best stop loss order price to use for the upcoming week, such that it will stay just below normal volatility, but high enough to provide a backstop exit price should the stock deviate from its normal level of volatility.

This stop loss formula is exceptionally accurate and will provide you with a consistently reliable stop loss price that will help protect your downside and yet give your stocks enough room to fluctuate in normal volatility actions.

VOLATILITY AND THE STOP LOSS PRICE

I have mentioned normal volatility several times. It is important that you clearly understand the importance and relationship between volatility and the stop loss price. Every stock has a fairly consistent pattern of volatility. Stocks do not, normally, go from a weekly price fluctuation of 5 percent that has been consistent for the past 12 months and then suddenly move into a consistent volatility pattern of 20 percent. One of the major assumptions behind this stop loss formula is that once a stock has established a normal level of volatility it will not abruptly change unless it is changing its pricing trend. This means a stock that is in an uptrend will stay in a consistent level of volatility as long as it continues in the uptrend.

Conversely, a stock will tend to stay within a consistent level of volatility when it is in a downtrend as long as that trend continues lower. Further, it is very likely that a stock will break out of a consistent volatility pattern when its pricing trend reverses, where uptrends move into downtrends and downtrends move into uptrends.

Statistically, we can calculate how much a stock is likely to move up or down (i.e., expected move), within one standard deviation of the mean of the past 12 months of a stock's volatility. The first step in determining the expected move (EM) is to calculate the historical volatility (HV):

$$HV = \frac{(52\,week\,high - 52\,week\,low)}{Average\,(52\,week\,high + weeek\,low)}$$

Once we have calculated the HV, we can next calculate the EM as follows:

Handwritten top margin:

For WRPSF on 3/29/19
EM= .07675
but WRPSF often moves .05 in 1 day
or .7 in 1 wk

$$EM = Stock\ Pr\ ice \times HV \times \left(\frac{\sqrt{5\ Trading\ Days}}{\sqrt{252\ Annual\ Trading\ Days}} \right)$$

Handwritten near formula: 2.236 / (15.8745) = .141

In the above formulas, the following definitions are applicable:

- The "Stock Price" is the most recent week-ending closing price.
- The "5 Trading Days" is the upcoming trading week. This means you are taking the square root of the number, "5".
- The "252 Annual Trading Days" represents the most recent 12 calendar months. This means you are taking the square root of the number, "252".

Handwritten: TXN: HV = .3   EM = 4.465

Handwritten: TXN Stop loss = 102.23

Once the EM has been calculated, you are then ready to calculate the best stop loss price for the upcoming trading week as follows:

Handwritten: FTNT Stop = 77.12   FTNT: HV = .578   EM = 6.85

STANDARD DEVIATION

Standard deviation is the root mean square (RMS) deviation of values from their arithmetic mean.

Handwritten: HRC: HV = .282   EM = 4.21   Stop = 101.65
ETSY: HV = .928   EM = 8.8   Stop = 58.42

- Stop loss for long positions = previous week's weekending closing price less the EM
- Stop loss for short positions = previous week's weekending closing price plus the EM

Handwritten: BLL: HV = .517   EM = 4.22   Stop = 53.64

There are several important observations and conclusions about this methodology that you should understand:

Handwritten: CME: HV = .246   EM = 5.71   Stop = 158.87

- Stop loss calculations are performed after the closing bell for the most recent week.
- The stop loss price is valid for the next trading week.
- Stop loss prices should be adjusted for known dividends/distributions that would cause the price of the stock to be adjusted by the amount of the dividend or distribution.

- If a stop loss calculation results in a price that is lower (in the case of long positions) than the previous week's stop loss price, the new stop loss price should remain at the previous level. In other words, do not lower your stop loss settings. For short positions, the opposite is true.
- For long positions, once the stop loss is higher than the top of the Transition Zone (see yellow band in Figure 5.3), then the stop loss becomes the top of the Transition Zone.
- For short positions, once the stop loss is lower than the bottom of the Transition Zone (see yellow band in Figure 5.3), then the stop loss becomes the bottom of the Transition Zone.

Let's look at an example.

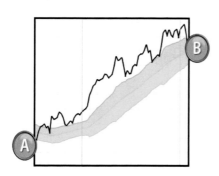

Figure 5.3

In this example (see), the week-ending price at Circle A crosses from inside Transition Zone (yellow band) to above the band. Assuming this is a stock or ETF that you want to own, this movement is considered a buy signal. You don't have to buy it here, but it is ok to buy, technically speaking. You will notice that the equity fluctuates significantly for months, but stays above the Transition Zone until it reaches Circle B.

If you purchased this stock immediately after it moved from inside to above the Transition Zone, the stop would be equal to the weekending close price less the EM. Then, as the stock's price would climb each week, you would raise the stop to be one EM below the Friday closing price, so long as the stop is not lowered at any time. You continue this process until the stop moves above the Transition Zone (see Figure 5.4).

Once the stop is at or above the Transition Zone, the top of the Transition Zone becomes the stop loss setting. Note the green dashed lines in Figure 5.4. These dashes represent the stop loss setting each week. You should notice that the stop loss started out below the top of the Transition Zone at Circle A, but eventually moved up to where the top of the Transition Zone becomes the stop.

As a reminder... the top of the Transition Zone is one EM above the 200-day moving average.

Finally, at Circle B, the stock's price dropped down to and through the top of the Transition Zone, and triggered the stop. You are probably wondering why the stop wasn't raised higher to capture more profit. I often raise stops well above the Transition Zone, but only for the purpose of going to cash. If I believe that the market has become overheated, as explained in the Market-Directional Methodology Chapter, I will raise stops and significantly

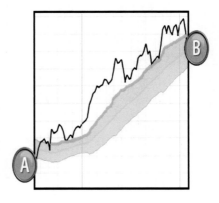

Figure 5.4

so. But please understand this: If you raise stops above the Transition Zone, you will significantly increase the likelihood of stopping out before you have to.

Back to the wildebeest analogy... As long as the herd is moving your stock's price in the right direction, you stay right in the middle of the herd. This would be, for example, between Circle A and Circle B. But when the herd moves in the wrong direction (see Circle B), you merely sell your shares and wait for a time when the herd once again starts pushing your stock from the lower left to the upper right.

What You Learned in This Rule

This is the "When to Sell" rule. In this rule, you learned:

- Why it is important to remove market and data noise from your thinking.
- That selling is far more important than buying.
- How and when to sell.
- How to completely remove the emotion of trying to guess the right time to sell a long position or cover a short position.
- How to calculate an expected move for each stock in your portfolio so you know when that stock has begun to exhibit pricing action that signals a change in direction and a potential new trend that could significantly erode your hard-earned, but unrealized, gains.
- Why using a stop loss is an essential investment strategy.
- How to calculate that stop loss without emotion or stress.
- How to let your stop loss settings be your exit strategy for each of your stocks.
- Most importantly, how to sleep at night without worrying about your stocks and that you can go on vacation again without constantly watching stock prices.

CHAPTER 6

THE ANTI-EMOTION RULE (FOR ADULTS ONLY!)

"Unrequited love is all you get from stocks!"

SMART TRADES + NO EMOTION = PROFITABLE RELATIONSHIPS

Let's review briefly. You've learned how to know whether you should have a bullish mindset or a bearish mindset or sitting on your hands. You have also learned how to think like a fundamentalist, how to use Demand Fundamentals to select only the best stocks, how to refine and narrow that "best list" of stocks by looking at relative value, how to time your entry point through the use of a simple but profoundly powerful technical analysis, and how to know when to sell through the use of an Intelligent Stop Loss® strategy.

In this Rule, you will learn to remove emotion from owning stocks. You will learn how to be agnostic about the holdings in your portfolio. Why do you suppose that so many investors (and this may very well include you) have an ongoing love affair with one or more of the stocks in their portfolio?

Don't get me wrong—love is a wonderful thing. You can love your spouse, your children, your grandchildren, your home, your work, your country, or even the stock market, like I do. You can love the fact that you may have made a lot of money in the stock market. But you should never, never love a stock.

MORE LOVE = LESS MONEY

There is an old saying that "love is blind." There is a *lot* of truth to that statement. Love tends to gloss over the blemishes and highlight the faintest glimmer of anything positive. Ask any mother, and she will tell you she has the most beautiful children. Ask any grandparent, and they will tell you they have the most incredible, intelligent, witty, handsome, and beautiful grandbabies in the world. (Well, at least mine are.) This is human nature and something that is wonderfully special about human beings. Unfortunately, this is a terrible quality to have when it comes to owning stock.

Too many times, investors become foolishly infatuated with a stock or a sector (how about those gold bugs) or an entire market. These investors become almost childish in their complete abandonment of common sense as they let emotion take over their investment life. This phenomenon is not restricted by age or gender or race. It can happen to the most sage, wizened and mature investors. When emotion takes over, mature judgment and reasoned investment strategies fall by the wayside.

As I have mentioned before, I get the opportunity to attend a number of investor-related events each year. During these events, I get into many different conversations with individual investors. Invariably, there will be someone who wants to know what I think about the current political machinations erupting from Washington, D.C. My wife, Sue, warns me before each of these investor meetings not to get into a political discussion with anyone. I try very hard to heed her advice. But, sometimes, an adept conversationalist will draw me into a discussion about why the current party in power is taking our country to "hell in a handbasket," and they want to make sure I agree with them.

This is kind of like asking a man if he has quit beating his wife. Regardless of his answer, he has made the wrong response. So it is with politics. Do I have a strong political opinion? Absolutely! Does that opinion change my investment methodology? Absolutely not! Nor should it change yours.

It doesn't matter what your political leaning is. It doesn't matter if your stock is helped or hurt by the current political climate. It doesn't matter if our current president is a genius or a buffoon. It doesn't matter if Congress is doing the right or the wrong thing. You should not let your political opinions make your emotions gain any control over your investment methodology. When that happens, you will start buying or selling based on emotions and not on a solid set of rules.

Likewise, it is a mistake for you to have an emotional opinion of a publicly traded company. You may have heard of a fairly famous and very successful stock market investor, Peter Lynch. One of his most famous investment strategies is to "invest in what you know." This, on the surface, seems to make a lot of sense, but in reality, it doesn't make any sense at all. You see, Mr. Lynch is like a lot of Wall Street professionals. They reason that the average, nonprofessional investor doesn't have time to learn complicated quantitative stock analysis methodologies and, as such, just can't compete with those of Mr. Lynch's ilk. Therefore, the poor nonprofessional investor must be relegated to investing in stocks of companies that the nonprofessional investor has some tangible experience with. You, the average nonprofessional investor must "invest in what you know" or else you are just guessing and really have no idea what you should or should not be buying in the way of stocks.

I submit to you that you can do far better with your stock investment dollars than most of the Wall Street "professionals" by depending on a solid set of investment rules, instead of an anecdotal and emotionally charged relationship you might have with a company's goods or services.

To "buy what you know" infers that your opinion of a company's goods and/or services means that the entire market has your same opinion. Just as in politics, you should not extrapolate your emotional opinions onto the public at large or the investor market for a particular stock. It is the epitome of arrogance to think that your opinion of a company's goods and services is the same view of an entire market. Buying "what you know" infers that if you like a product, you should like the company that produces that product, and that you should, therefore, buy stock because of your emotional attachment to the company behind that stock.

The Peter Lynches of the world can assume that you, the lowly non-professional can never compete in the professional world of stock investing and must rely on your emotions to pick stocks, but they are wrong. In this day and age, you have *all* the requisite access to financial information to have a rules-based quantitative investment methodology that is *not* tied to emotions. You have the ability to create an investment strategy that can and will produce consistent and significant profits in the stock market, and do so without emotional attachments.

My point in all of this is that you must strive to eliminate emotions from your investment strategy, even when the Wall Street moguls tell you that emotional investing is the best you can do. You've heard the talking heads on CNBC say, "if you like a certain product, then buy the stock." That kind of talk is simply asinine. You don't want to invest your money in a stock simply because you like the products that the company produces. You are not the market. Your purchase of shares will not change the supply/demand curve for shares of the company. You want to invest money into shares of a stock that has the likelihood to move higher in price whether you like the company or not or whether you like the company's products or not.

Another reason to keep emotion out of your investment methodology is that emotion ignores common sense. Without common sense guiding your investments, you might as well be tossing a coin to make buying and selling decisions. Emotional investing is the worst kind of investing. It is the same thing as blind investing.

Emotional trading will cause you to be unduly influenced from past entanglements with the company, such as liking their products or the amount of money you have made with that company in the past, or even a negative experience you have had with that company in the past. You must be very careful to avoid letting emotions and/or historical experiences with a company rule the day when it comes to decision-making. Buying, selling, shorting, or covering is a decision that should be based on the merits of the event itself. Strive to ignore past investments, losses, or gains, in a stock. Treat every trade as if it is the first trade you have ever made. View each trade from the perspective of what you gain from the trade, not what that trade has done in your past.

LEAVING THE PAST BEHIND

Let's pretend you bought 10,000 shares of XYZ for $200 per share. This would be a $2 million investment into XYZ stock. For most of us, putting $2 million dollars into a single stock would be considered a significant investment. But you don't care. You *love* the XYZ Corporation. You love their products. You believe that the founder of the company is a giant among his peers. You are so proud of your $2 million dollar investment into XYZ! Hopefully, by now, you can see how wrong it is to be investing in any company based on a love affair with the company, its products, or its management personnel. But, just to drive this point home, I am going to continue with the scenario.

Now, let's say XYZ begins to move lower in price. Let's pretend it moves lower by 10 percent. If you were following the Stop Loss Rule, you would have likely already stopped out. At this writing, the stop loss for XYZ is about 8.19 percent below last week's lowest low. So, at a 10 percent pullback, you would have sold XYZ.

But you look at how much money you would lose if you sold and realize that would cost you a whopping $200,000. That's a *lot* of money. Plus, you still love XYZ and you are convinced that the XYZ stock will soon recover. You're not going to give up on that investment for just 10 percent!

Then the XYZ stock moves down another 20 percent. You are now showing a paper loss of $600,000! You are not happy about the stock's market price and start thinking evil thoughts about the people out there that are pushing XYZ's stock lower. They are all just a bunch of market manipulators and the worst of the lot are the short sellers of XYZ!

You can't possibly sell now. You have invested too much money into the XYZ position and cannot face the real loss of $600,000. So you hold on, hoping the stock will someday recover. It might—or it might go even lower. There were many people who thought the same thing about Enron several years ago.

If you had not had such a love affair with XYZ and the impact of losing $200,000, you would have been out of XYZ with a loss of 8 percent or so. Now, you are facing a loss of more than 30 percent and still can't manage to get away from your emotional and financial tie to the XYZ stock.

It is times like these when an investor quits thinking about cutting losses or preserving capital and blindly plunges forward, believing (or hoping) that only good things can happen in the future. They blindly marry into a stock or a company and are convinced the marriage will last forever. Unfortunately, reality will set in sooner or later. I am reminded of an old country music song that had the following, para-phrased, lyrics: "I went to bed with a 10 and woke up with a 2!" This is a story that has more truth in it than many investors want to admit.

In the above example, you married and went to bed with a stock that represented the best company in the world—a "10." Now, down more than 30 percent and still dropping, you have come to realize that you woke up with a disaster—a "2." That's what happens when you marry a stock and fall in love with an inanimate object that can *never* love you back!

So...Are You Married to a Stock?

I like to say, "Never marry a stock because you won't like the divorce!"

Here are some ways you can tell if you are married to a stock, and what to do about it:

- *You love the dividend.* You bought this stock when it was selling for less than $2 and now it is trading at $60, and its dividend yield at current prices is 4%, but that equates to 120% due to your basis in the stock. You see no reason to ever sell this stock. Although there may be a very good reason to own a stock, it still does not justify taking the position of never wanting to sell. You are so in love with this stock that you are blinded by the relative yield. The fact that a company has paid a dividend for decades does not mean it will always pay a dividend. Plus, no company is totally immune from going out of business. Toys R Us was in business for over 70 years before going bankrupt. Even with the scenario described above, you should seriously consider what it would take for you to sell that stock. Then, set your stop loss or exit strategy accordingly.

- *You love the products that the company makes.* You are a part of their culture and you feel proud to own shares in this company. You carry their products in your pocket, or have it sitting on your kitchen counter. You have seen this company struggle against far stronger and better-capitalized competitors, and yet this company has prevailed. When you think about the shares of stock you hold in this company, you have a warm, glowing feeling about your commitment to them. You are definitely married to this stock!

Companies are businesses, not emotional beings. The mandate of the company is to build shareholder value, and regardless of how you may think otherwise, the ultimate success or failure of the company is measured in return on equity. A company has no feelings. It has no emotion. Companies do not have souls. Companies are business entities run by human beings. This company does not care about your hopes and aspirations. It does not care that you are trying to provide for your family. When this company's board meets, they do not discuss how close you are to achieving your goals for retirement. They do not think about you in the least, other than as a minuscule statistical component of their millions of shareholders. You may love your stock in this company, but your love is definitely unrequited.

- *You did a lot of research on this company before buying its stock.* You love their management style. You were convinced your investment would pay off handsomely. After you invested a substantial amount of your life's savings into this company, its stock went higher and higher and higher still. You were so proud of your investment prowess. You bragged to your friends about how smart you were to buy in just when you did. Thinking about this investment made you smile. Then, the stock began to trade lower and lower and lower still. At one point, you had lost all your one-time profits and were down more than 30%. You couldn't stand it any longer. Your only hope was to cut your cost basis in half. You knew that if you doubled the number of shares you own, you could cut your 30% loss to just 15%. What did you do? You doubled the number of shares you had by buying more, with the *hope* that the stock would rebound enough for you to get out. But it didn't move higher. It moved even lower. You hate this stock, now. You wish you had never bought it. You want out, but you can't leave—you are married to this stock, so you hang on, hoping that one day it will recover to some of its glory days.

This is a tragic story that is repeated all too often by thousands of investors. You are emotionally tied to the fear of losing money and admitting that you made three terrible mistakes: You made the mistake of <u>buying</u> the stock; you made the mistake of <u>not selling</u> when it had gone up so much; and you made the mistake of <u>buying more</u> of such a loser. You are in a death spiral and don't know how to get out.

Actually, this divorce is easier to resolve than most. Just ask yourself this question: If you had the cash instead of the shares, would you buy the stock now? If the answer is yes, then hold onto it. If the answer is no, then sell it. In either case, use the Stop Loss Rule to set your stop loss.

- *Many investors believe that if they own shares of stock in a company, they actually own part of the company.* This might be legally true, but it is completely false in practical application. Sure, if you own a huge percentage of a company's outstanding shares you can have some influence with the company's management, but you still don't own the company. You don't actually own the assets of the company. You don't have any liability for their debts. You merely own a piece of paper that represents a small percentage of "control" of the company. But even if you own a lot of shares, you still can't control the company. Don't believe me? Here is a test for you that will prove it to you. The next time a company declares that it is going bankrupt, buy some shares of the company and see how much you get back when the company is liquidated. You will get nothing. The shareholder stock does not provide you with actual, physical ownership of any assets of the company. One hundred percent of the assets of the company belong to the company, not the shareholders. The only people who ever get anything back from a company that is liquidated are the creditors, and oftentimes, they don't get anything either. So, don't fool yourself into thinking that when you buy shares of stock you are buying ownership in a company. You are not. You are only buying ownership in shares of stock. Those shares of stock only have value if there is a market for those shares. Otherwise, they are worth less than the paper they are printed on.

The simple implementation of this Rule is never to get married to a stock. Being emotionally attached to stocks will always lead you down the path of this pseudo-marriage.

Regardless of how long you have held a stock and regardless of how low your basis and regardless of your current financial condition, you *must* have an exit strategy for every stock in your portfolio.

You should sit down right now and put a price (e.g., stop loss order) on every stock in your portfolio. Ask yourself this question: "Is there any price that would cause me to believe it is a good time to sell?" If you cannot come up with a price, then you should consider that you are so emotionally tied to the stock and are at risk of losing everything you have in that stock. Don't believe me? History shows that one of the largest banks in the world (Bear Stearns) went from being worth $160 per share to only $2 per share in a few months. Indeed, at the end, this same company went from being worth $50 per share to $2 per share in less than three days.

This should NOT happen to you!

How to Avoid Falling in Love with a Stock

You do not have to let your emotions rule your investing methodology and strategy. There is a simple way to keep your emotions in check. Here is how:

1. Develop a solid set of rules to follow for making stock market trading decisions. These 10 Essential Rules are an excellent set of rules that will work for any investor.
2. Don't violate your rules regardless of what your emotions tell you. Gut instinct is good, but it should be used to help you build your rules, not steer your stock selections.
3. Finally, keep this in the forefront of your mind when it comes to making consistent profits in the stock market: **Your *rules* should completely govern how you invest in the stock market, but *you* should completely govern your rules.** When it comes to the decision-making process for stock market investing, follow your rules zealously!

WHAT YOU LEARNED IN THIS RULE

In this "adults-only" rule, you learned:

- Why it is important to not let the past overly influence your trading decisions.
- How to know if you are married to a stock.
- Why it is wrong and can be devastatingly expensive to be married to a stock, especially when you are served divorce papers by your stock.
- How to avoid being married to a stock.
- That following a good set of rules will help you process through the emotions of owning a stock.

CHAPTER 7

THE INSIDER BUYING RULE

"Monitoring insider selling is a total waste of time!"

STRONG FUNDAMENTALS + BOTTOMING TECHNICALS + INSIDER BUYING = HUGE UPSIDE POTENTIAL

B y the time you get to this rule, you are well on your way to knowing how to find the best stocks to own, when to buy them, and when to sell them. You also know how to avoid getting emotionally attached to your stocks.

Now, it is time to start doing a little refining of your growing and evolving investment strategy. Let's move on to see what we can glean from insider trading.

In this Rule, you will learn how to analyze legal insider trading and how to use the data to help you make a final, perhaps critical, decision on selecting and/or ranking the stocks that you may consider adding to your portfolio. Finding the right stock that fits all of your requirements for buying out of many thousands of stocks is truly akin to finding a needle in a haystack. We want to narrow that search down to just a handful of the best of the best. We will do that by using insider trading data, but we'll use only one very specific type of insider trading data.

What Is Insider Trading?

Insider trading is a term that most investors have heard and usually associate with illegal activities. But the term actually includes both legal and illegal conduct. The legal version is when corporate insiders—officers, directors, and employees—buy and sell stock in their own companies. When corporate insiders trade in their own securities, they must report their trades to the Securities and Exchange Commission (SEC).

Illegal insider trading refers generally to buying or selling a security, in breach of a fiduciary duty or other relationship of trust and confidence, while in possession of significant nonpublic information about the security. Insider trading violations may also include "tipping" such information, securities trading by the person "tipped," and securities trading by those who misappropriate such information.

Insider trading is illegal only when a person bases his or her trade on information that is unavailable to the public. It is also illegal to give insider information to another person, whereby that person makes equity trades based on that information. There is very little illegal insider trading since those who practice it are so easily caught and almost always face significant fines and jail time. For example, Martha Stewart was convicted of lying to the SEC regarding insider trading information. She was told by her friend Sam Waksal that his company's (ImClone) cancer drug had been rejected by the Food and Drug Administration (FDA) before this information was made public. The rejection by the FDA was very damaging to the company and resulted in a dramatic drop in share price. However, Martha Stewart avoided this drop in share price because she sold her shares before the FDA news was made public.

Martha Stewart

Martha Stewart is an American business magnate, author, editor, and homemaking advocate. She is also a former stockbroker and fashion model. Stewart has held a prominent position in the American publishing industry as the author of several books and hundreds of articles on the domestic arts, editor of a national housekeeping magazine, host of two daytime television programs, and commercial spokeswoman for K-mart. In 2001 she was named the third most powerful woman in America by *Ladies Home Journal.* In 2004 she was convicted of lying to investigators about a stock sale and served five months in prison.

SAMUEL D. WAKSAL

Samuel D. Waksal founded the biopharmaceutical company ImClone Systems in 1984. He was arrested on June 12, 2002, on insider trading charges, and subsequently pleaded guilty to charges of securities fraud, bank fraud, obstruction of justice, and perjury.

SOME INSIDER TRADING IS GREAT NEWS

On the legal side of insider trading, there are two trades that can occur: insider selling and insider buying. Let's just deal with the legal side. A lot of investors think that *insider selling* is important information to know.

When I speak to large audiences, while the room is filling up, I like to chat with the audience and get to know them a little better and to give the audience an opportunity to warm to my presentation style of speaking. A question that I often ask is, "Could I see a show of hands of everyone who believes it is important for investors to monitor insider selling?"

I am always surprised at how many hands go up, although each year there seems to be fewer and fewer, which is a good thing.

Many investors seem to think that if an insider is selling, it must be because the insider knows the company is doing poorly or will soon have problems. This is almost always *not* the case because if an insider sells on this information, that person is committing a felony. There are hundreds of reasons for insider selling. Here are just a few:

- The insider is required to exercise stock options and must sell stock to pay for the options.

- The insider needs money to pay for his/her children's college education.
- The insider needs to pay off major medical bills.
- The insider wants to diversify his/her portfolio and owns too much of the company's stock and, therefore, must sell shares.
- The insider owns too much of the company's stock and, due to the requirements of an upcoming merger, the insider is required to divest (sell) a significant portion of his/her shares in order for the merger to take place.
- The insider wants to buy a second home or pay off the mortgage on his/her first home.

In fact, more times than not, when insiders sell, it is likely that the company is doing well and will do well in the future. I know that sounds counterintuitive, so let me explain.

Because insider trading is so highly scrutinized by the SEC and because there is the potential for serious consequences regarding illegal trading, many corporate insiders wait until there is not even the hint of bad news on the horizon before selling shares. Insiders can be somewhat paranoid about selling shares at any time, since it is possible for bad news to come out later on the company. Even if they didn't know about the news in advance, they will likely be investigated and accused of trading on insider knowledge.

This is why many executives have a preset formula for selling shares so that they can rightly claim that the selling of shares was predetermined by formula and had nothing to do with insider knowledge.

So, with this in mind, my philosophy is to *ignore insider selling*.

However, there is only *one* reason for insider buying: The insider believes the stock in the company is cheap compared to where it should be. Insider buying can also be deemed illegal if the insider is buying stock based on information not available to the public. But, insiders have the opportunity to look at the company from the inside out. No one is likely to know better about the health and future growth of the company than an insider. When an insider buys, it is almost always a very good indication that good things are more likely on the horizon for the company, rather than bad things.

How to Use Insider Buying Information

When you have several stocks that are otherwise equal in quality and opportunity for pricing growth and you are trying to decide which is the better stock to buy, always look at the insider buying.

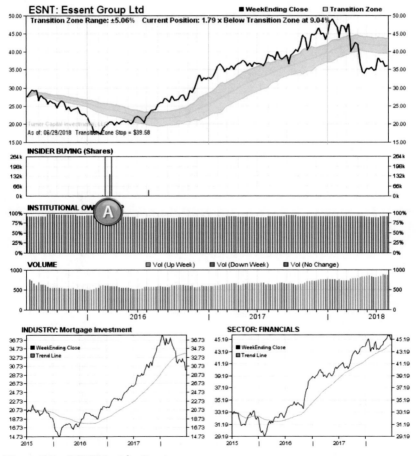

Figure 7.1—ESNT Insider Buying

Figure 7.1 shows an example chart of stock that which, at the time of this writing, was a Demand Fundamental buy-rated stock, according the Fundamentals Rule. But at the same time this stock was buy-rated, there were more than 150 other stocks that were also buy-rated, among the 6,000 stocks that I track at any one time.

When I begin narrowing down my list of stocks to buy, one of the major criteria that I consider is insider buying. I consider it a very big plus when a stock that I am considering buying has a recent record of strong insider buying.

Take a look at Circle A in Figure 7.1. Notice how the significant increase in insider buying coincides with a low point in the stock's market price. But what is so very important and often very typical is the directional move of the stock's pricing trend in the months that followed that strong level of insider buying. The stock went on a multi-month run, with the market price of shares moving nicely from the lower left to the upper right.

When you are looking to add a new position to your portfolio, you want as many positive, growth-oriented activities as possible supporting your trade. It is almost never a good idea to be a loner when it comes to buying stocks. It is far better to be in with the crowd that is pushing your stock's price higher and higher. So when you are trying to make a final decision on which stock, look at buying alongside the insiders.

But as with the other rules in this book, do not use insider buying as the *only* criterion for buying a stock. When I am considering a new stock to buy, insider buying is one of the last things that I consider, not one of the first.

Look back at Figure 7.1. There are many reasons to buy this stock once the price moves above the Transition Zone, not the least of which is insider buying a few months earlier. The trading volume was strong, which is a very good sign. The industry was moving into bull mode, which was extremely positive and supported buying the stock. The sector was also moving higher.

Every technical indicator was positive, including insider buying. With the Demand Fundamental supporting the trade and the technicals supporting the trade, this stock was certainly one of those screaming buy situations, but ONLY after the week-ending price moved above the Transition Zone.

I hope you see how clearly you can arrive at a decision to buy or sell with this methodology. You don't have to read bulletin boards, analyst reviews, trade journals, and financial newsletters, or listen to talking heads on TV to know exactly when to buy and exactly when to sell with this methodology.

By this point, you should begin to see how you can take control of your stock market investment strategy and know exactly what to do in all markets and at all times!

WHAT YOU LEARNED IN THIS RULE

In this rule on insider trading, you learned:

- Why insider selling data is virtually irrelevant when considering whether to enter into or exit out of a stock holding.
- Why insider buying can provide great insight into the next several months of the performance of the stock's share price.
- That the first step in making consistent profits in the market requires making good stock selections from the entire universe of stocks. At any given time, there are likely to be dozens (sometimes hundreds) of stocks that have great fundamentals and great technicals and are efficiently priced—many more stocks than you could buy even if you wanted to. It is at times like these that you must have criteria for screening the best of the best from the group of potentially great trades. Sometimes, only insider buying data will give you that edge to make your final selection.

CHAPTER 8

THE INSTITUTIONAL OWNERSHIP RULE

"Contrary to what you hear on TV every day, there are no undiscovered stocks, so put your shovel down and stop digging for them!"

STRONG FUNDAMENTALS +
STRONG TECHNICALS +
MODERATE INSTITUTIONAL OWNERSHIP = ODDS OF SUCCESSFUL TRADE INCREASE

In the Market-Directional Methodology Chapter, you learned that unless the market is moving with you, the best course of action is to do no buying and no shorting. You've learned several trading rules to this point, including how to use fundamentals, technicals, PE ratios, Stop Loss settings and Insider Buying. You have mastered how to avoid emotional entanglements with stocks.

This Rule is another stock selection refinement rule. Here, you will learn how to use institutional ownership as another important element for finding just the right stock to buy at the right time.

Think with me for a moment. What if I told you that all the big name institutional investors were going to put the combined resources of all their corporate research staffs together to find the very best companies with the best management teams, the best products, the best growth plans, the best products in the pipeline, the most undervalued, and the ones with the highest likelihood of their stock price moving significantly higher? And when they complete this monumental task of analysis, and after they have narrowed their list down to just the few that they really want to own, they are going to call you up and tell you which companies that they have selected?

Do you think you could use this kind of information?

Amazingly, this is exactly what large institutions have to do. They have to report to the public exactly what they own and whether they have recently bought or sold shares in each company that they have traded. It's the law, and this information is available to you for *free*!

But before I get into the details about how to make the most out of this information, let's see why this information is so valuable to us.

DON'T BE MISLED

Some TV personalities and so-called financial experts will tell you that if you just listen to them or if you just "do your homework," you will find that next big "undiscovered" company. They want you to believe that you can find the next Microsoft or Apple; or worse, they want you to believe that if you will just listen to them, they will tell you something that "Wall Street" hasn't found yet. Of course, they want you to believe that you can "get in on the ground floor" and buy shares now before the big know-it-all Wall Street types can figure it out.

This is simply delusional and silly, at best. At worst, it is just a big lie.

I hate to break it to you, but for *individual investors*, there just are no undiscovered companies. By the time we think we have found an undiscovered jewel that is going to skyrocket as soon as Wall Street finds the company, Wall Street has already vetted the company and either bought or passed on the shares of the stock.

As individual investors, we don't have the manpower to peruse through the voluminous amount of data it would require to gain such information before the big institutions can find these undiscovered companies.

VETTED

Evaluated for possible approval or acceptance.

Big institutional investors have rooms full of MBAs who have only one job in life—to find undiscovered companies. Major institutional investors have the resources and time to seek out and analyze every publicly traded company. If they find a winner, they buy in. They take a "pass" on all the other companies that don't meet their criteria for growth and quality.

To think that Wall Street has somehow missed a company, or that somehow you, as an individual investor, can find an undiscovered company before the big institutional investors find that company is just wrong thinking. If the staffs of major institutional investors somehow miss a real gem of a company, heads will roll. People will be fired. No, every company that is worth owning has already been vetted by one or more of the big players on Wall Street, regardless of what you may have heard otherwise.

THE PROBLEMS OF BEING A MAJOR INSTITUTION

I am going to ask you to step into the shoes of a portfolio manager of a major institution. Your job is to find ways to invest in the stock market the billions of dollars held by the institution. And your job is on the line if you screw this up!

What's more, you have to report to the public exactly how you invested this money each quarter, so it puts even more pressure on you to make sure you pick the right stocks.

The good news is that you have a very large budget for research staff. You can hire anyone you want and buy all the research data you want.

So you hire yourself a bunch of new MBA graduates, give them access to all available corporate research, and on top of all of that, you put together a field staff that is required to make on-site visits to every company your research staff tell you is a potential candidate for your portfolio.

Now, keep in mind that you have several billions of dollars and, as such, you have to look everywhere possible for companies to invest in. You never have enough good companies for the amount of money you have, so you continually put pressure on your research staffs to make sure not a single company is missed. They must scrutinize all public companies.

And every few days, your boss and your boss's boss come in to see why you aren't making them higher returns. This is really a high-pressure job!

DON'T BELIEVE THE WALL STREET TITANS

You know, the arrogance of big name Wall Street investors never ceases to amaze me, and it doesn't matter if they live in Omaha, Nebraska or New York. They all seem to look down their noses at individual investors and tell them with some veiled disdain that there is no way that you, the lowly individual investor, can compete with their big money, big staffs, and almost infinite knowledge of the market and financial investing.

Don't you believe them! You not only can compete with these titans, but when it comes to net total return, you can outperform most of them most of the time. Warren Buffett may be happy with an 8% return on billions of dollars, but your return can do much better and, by the way, avoid the massive losses that BRK-A endures every few years.

These rules will put you on a course to outperform these Wall Street "titans." One reason is that you don't have to invest millions or billions of dollars at a time. You can afford to own smaller chunks of stock, and you can be much quicker on your feet—meaning you can get in and out of a trade very quickly without worrying about the size of the trade and amount of money that will have to change hands.

Plus, you have access to enough information to make very informed and unbiased decisions about which stocks you will buy and when you sell. It is very, very unlikely that Warren Buffett has or needs a stop loss strategy. He can't afford to make decisions that quickly, but you can. The big titans of Wall Street have access to huge quantities of information on every market and every company in the world. You don't have that data, but you do have the results of that data by watching what companies the big institutions select for investment. Having access to the end results of institutional trading is just another way you can play on the same field as the biggest investors in the world when it comes to buying and selling stocks of publicly traded companies.

You may not have a room full of MBA graduates doing research for you, but you certainly can get access to the end results of all that institutional research data. And you can put that knowledge to great use. You have everything you need. You just need to know how to tap into this knowledge. Let me show you how.

How to Use Institutional Trading

If these big institutional investors are already doing the hard work of finding all the undiscovered companies—all the companies worth owing—how does an individual investor tap into all of that knowledge and investment research data? And how much will it cost you to obtain that information? You might be thinking, "Oh, if I could just peek over the fence to see what they are getting ready to buy." Well, it may surprise you, but, indeed, you can do just that!

Institutional Ownership

Institutional ownership refers to the total number of shares of publicly traded companies that are held (owned) by large financial organizations, pension funds, or endowments.

Here's the good news: **There is really only one piece of information you need to know from these big institutions, and that is the *percentage* of ownership that they have in publicly traded companies.**

If institutional investors find a great company, they buy shares in that company, and they have to *report* their ownership to the public.

Finding that information is wonderfully simple. It is available for free. All you have to do is get on Yahoo! or MSN or Google or any web site that provides stock market data and you can find the total number of institutional investors and the percentage of the outstanding shares they own for every publicly traded company.

Think of it this way: Remember when I asked you to pretend you are the portfolio manager of a big institution earlier in this chapter? Imagine you have just arrived at work. You go to your corner office. Your assistant has your day's agenda. The financial newspapers are all on your desk. But the most important report on your desk are the results from your research staff. They have worked around the clock to provide you with a list of companies you should consider buying.

You make your decision and place your stock orders.

Now, a few weeks later, you have to report to the world what you own and how many shares you own. That's when you and I can peek over the fence.

That's when we know the results of all that expensive research.

If the results of the data recommend increasing ownership in a publicly traded company, then these big institutions will be buying more shares. If the results are negative, they will not be buying, or will even divest themselves of shares.

Watching and tracking the trading habits of big institutions as they increase or decrease their ownership in publicly traded companies is an excellent way to use the resources of their research departments. It *is* like peeking over the fence!

YOU CAN NOT ONLY LOOK OVER THE FENCE— YOU CAN HOP OVER IT!

Charting institutional ownership is a very good way to see trends that you can use to your advantage. It is also a great way to visually and rapidly determine if the institutional ownership is too light or too strong.

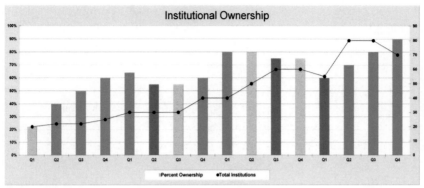

Figure 8.1

Figure 8.1 is an example of a chart that I have used to track institutional ownership for XYZ Company.

There is, surprisingly, quite a bit of useful information in a chart like this. Let's see what this has to tell us.

The vertical bars represent the total percentage of outstanding shares owned by large institutions. This means that of all the shares available on the open market for XYZ Company, 20% are owned by large institutions. This is a very good sign that at least some institutions have vetted XYZ Company and have come away believing the company is solid, from a fundamental perspective, and its share price is likely to be increasing in the near future.

You will also notice that there is a black line on the Figure 8.1 chart. This black line represents the number of large institutions who own shares of XYZ Company. The more large institutions that buy shares in a company, the better—to a point (more on this later).

You want to see, over time, that big institutions are buying more shares and that more institutions are buying into the company. Increasing institutional involvement in the company means that the word is spreading that the future is bright and growing brighter. Share prices should be increasing.

You can quickly see from a chart like the one in Figure 8.1 whether big institutions own any shares in XYZ Company. With no vertical bars, the institutional ownership would be zero.

You can see if XYZ Company stock is "under accumulation" if the vertical bars become taller from one quarter to the next. A stock that is being accumulated by large institutions is a very good indicator of future growth in the company. The institutions have analyzed the company and believe the company will grow, and therefore, the share price will increase.

Likewise, if the stock is "under distribution," the vertical bars become shorter from one quarter to the next. A stock that is under distribution by large institutions means that the future growth of the company is not as strong as in the past. Institutions have analyzed the company and believe the company will grow, but not as fast as before, and the likelihood of the share price's increasing is not quite as strong as before.

Under Accumulation

"Under accumulation" means that, over time, more shares are being purchased and held by the buyer. Generally, this is construed to be a very bullish indicator on the stock being accumulated, and it is likely that the stock's market share price will be increasing in the near future.

If large institutions believe the company's stock will begin to move much lower because the future growth potential of the company is very negative, the institutions will bail out, often en masse.

A stock that is under distribution (being sold) is not a good sign if your objective is to be long in the stock. It is a great sign if you plan to short the stock. When a stock is under distribution, it means that large institutions have decided the company is overweighted in their portfolios and they are divesting (selling) shares.

Under Distribution

"Under Distribution" means that, over time, fewer shares are held by the holder as more and more shares are sold. Generally, this is construed to be a negative indicator on the stock, and it is likely that the stock's market share price will be decreasing in the near future.

Monitoring the total number of institutional owners is also a good indicator of future share price movement—the more institutional owners, the better, for upward pricing movement.

OVERWEIGHTED

Institutions have more of a particular company than they want to own.

HOW TO INTERPRET INSTITUTIONAL OWNERSHIP

When making a decision on which stock to buy or short, institutional ownership can provide you with some critically important insight. It is important to understand the impact of institutional ownership and whether that ownership helps or hurts your ability to generate a profit from the stock you are considering for purchase.

The following are some key elements to consider when analyzing institutional ownership:

- A company that has no institutional ownership is a negative indicator. This means that big institutions have analyzed the company and have decided to pass on any ownership. Major institutions have huge sums of money to invest, so they are always looking for good opportunities. If there is not significant institutional participation in a stock, then it is probably not the best stock selection for a long position. Another way to think about this is to recall our wildebeest herd analogy. In this case, the herd is the collective world of big institutions. If your stock is *not* in the middle of the herd and moving from lower left to upper right (in this case, the analogy would be "shares under accumulation"), then you should seriously consider not buying this stock. Keep in mind that I will on occasion buy a stock that is not owned by any major institutions, but the Demand Fundamentals, the industry and sector charts, the directional move on average trading volume, and the stock's technical chart *must* be overwhelmingly compelling.
- One of the objectives of big institutions is to do all they can to drive up share price in their portfolio companies. So, institutional ownership is a good thing when it comes to

analyzing a potential addition to your portfolio. It is good to buy stocks that have institutional ownership. It is better to buy stocks that have an upward trend in the percentage ownership by institutional investors. You want to see shares under accumulation. Referring back to Figure 8.1, you want to see the vertical bars getting taller and taller. And you want to see the number of institutions holding shares in your stock increasing from one quarter to the next.

- There is a downside to institutional ownership when institutions own too many of the outstanding shares of a company. When institutions decide to sell or divest themselves of ownership in a company, they tend to sell very large numbers of shares. And it is not uncommon that when one institution starts selling, others will follow in rapid succession. This is the wildebeest herd. Remember, when they turn and start running in another direction, the whole herd turns. Soon, there can be a huge sell-off in a stock when nothing in particular has happened to the company. But, when this sell-off happens, the share price can plummet if institutions own too much of the company. For example, if institutions own 20% of the outstanding shares, the impact of a 5% sell-off by institutions is significant, but not overwhelming. However, if institutions own 98% of the outstanding shares, a 5% sell-off can have a huge impact on share price and can lead to a 10% or 20% reduction in share price, once the selling begins.

- I have found the following to be very good rules of thumb when it comes to institutional ownership:

1. Consider it a negative if there is less than 5% institutional ownership in a company. This does not prohibit you from buying shares in the company, but it is a negative that you should weigh when making your final stock selection. Buying a stock with less than 5% institutional ownership adds a little risk to your investment.

2. Consider it a negative if there is more than 95% institutional ownership in a company. Again, this does not prohibit you from buying shares in the company, but it is a big negative, especially if you eventually accumulate a lot of unrealized gain in your stock. An institutional bailout could wipe out your gains in a matter of seconds. So buying a stock with 95% or more institutional ownership adds quite a bit of risk to your investment.

3. Stocks that have between 30% and 60% institutional ownership are considered in my "sweet spot." These are stocks that have been seriously vetted by several big institutions and have impressed their research staffs sufficiently to cause some serious investment in their stocks by large institutions. At the same time, the big institutions do not own so much of the outstanding shares as to force a pricing collapse if they decide to sell.

WHAT YOU LEARNED IN THIS RULE

In this rule, you learned:

- Why watching large institutions buy and sell stock in publicly traded companies should be an important component of your investment strategy.
- That a good rule of thumb is to avoid stocks that have institutional ownership of less than 5% or more than 95%.
- **That the sweet spot for institutional ownership is 30% to 60%.**
- That it is very important to understand that this Rule is not to be taken as the only criterion for selecting a stock. It is just another of the rules in this book that is intended to help you choose between two stocks that are, in all other ways, identical in fundamentals and technicals.

But, when you have to make a final selection from a very small group of stocks under your consideration, you should use institutional ownership as one way to make your final selection.

CHAPTER 9

THE DIVERSIFICATION RULE

*"If you always assume the worst is possible, you will
never be surprised."*

BALANCED INDUSTRIES +
BALANCED SECTORS =
BALANCED LOWER RISK PORTFOLIO

At this point, you have learned how to know when to be in the
market, how to use fundamentals and technicals to find the right
stock at the right time to buy. You have learned how to set an exit strategy and not to get emotionally attached to a stock. You have learned how
to use insider buying and institutional ownership to further refine your
stock selection process.

But if all you do is find the right stocks to buy at the right time, you
can still fail (and fail miserably) at building a world-class portfolio of
stocks. This Rule and the Asset Allocation Rule will teach you how to
balance your investments based on the amount of money you have to
invest in the stock market and, at the same time, avoid putting too many
of your eggs in one basket.

This Rule is all about diversification. In this Rule, you will learn how
proper diversification can save your investment life when all else fails.

Do Not Put All Your Eggs in One Basket

You have heard all your life that you shouldn't put all your eggs in one basket. In other words, you should not put your entire life's financial security into a single investment or single type of investment. The reason is obvious, of course. The risk is just too high that something unforeseen could happen and either financially cripple you or, worse, wipe you out completely.

I doubt there are very many investors who do not clearly recognize the truth in that saying. But you might be surprised at how few investors do much more than pay lip service to this axiom of life.

It amazes me how most investors either do not know how to stay diversified or they simply believe the worst cannot happen to them. I was at a meeting recently where I was extolling the importance of a sensible, rules-based approach to diversification. From the back of the room, a gentleman raised his hand and said that well-diversified portfolios couldn't make enough profit for him. He went on to say that he purposely keeps his portfolio undiversified.

I'll admit that his remarks surprised me. I'm sure a lot of investors may think that, but it is rare to hear someone actually proclaim it as a strategy.

My response to him was that I place too high a value on low risk and that I am quite satisfied to make market-beating returns with highly diversified portfolios. I could tell from his body language that he was skeptical. I wasn't sure if his skepticism was about the market-beating returns or the risk comment.

It is possible that you can be lucky and bet the farm on a single strategy that pays off in huge returns. But do you really want to "bet the farm" when the "farm" is your entire financial life? I don't know of anyone willing to put everything at risk on one spin of the roulette wheel. Because that is exactly what it is—gambling. A poorly diversified portfolio is virtually the same as turning your portfolio into a game of chance.

Stock market investing is *not* gambling if you are a rules-based investor and follow a regimented and disciplined investment strategy. However, if you guess at what to buy and when to sell and ignore diversification, you would likely be just as well off to go to Vegas and play the gambling tables.

Smart diversification can turn your investments into money-making strategies. Lack of diversification will turn your investments into a game of chance.

Let me illustrate what I mean.

There was a time when owning REITs (real estate investment trusts) was almost the same thing as printing money. In fact, REITs were doing so well that you could hardly lose money, regardless of which REIT you would buy. They were all surging higher in share price almost every day. Several of these REITs hadn't triggered a sell signal for more than two years!

It became a no-brainer to have more and more REITs in your portfolio. And, it wasn't long before REITs became the majority holding in many individual investor portfolios. Some had invested so much in REITs that REITs made up more than 60% of their portfolio. It wasn't uncommon to make more than 6% and sometimes more than 10% gains in these portfolios on a weekly basis. These investors, who gave no thought to diversification, looked like geniuses! They were bragging about their investment savvy and constantly talked about their massive returns!

REIT

A real estate investment trust that purchases and manages property and/or mortgage loans. REITs are traded just like stocks.

Well, I am sure you know what happened to those investors who were so heavily over-loaded in the REIT industry. The bottom fell out of the REIT industry. Some REITs lost more than 40% within a matter of hours. It was not uncommon to see those undiversified portfolios tumble lower by more than 20% in just a few days' time. Months and years of profit vanished in the blink of an eye.

I believe in being a good steward of your financial resources. There is no excuse for managing an undiversified portfolio. Generally, when a portfolio gets over-loaded in one Sector or Industry, it is due to lack of discipline, or too much ego or simple complacency. Betting the farm on too few investment choices almost always leads to financial ruin.

You must learn that unrealized gain is a fleeting mistress that looks real one moment and vaporizes the next. Experience is a cruel and harsh teacher. Better that you learn this lesson here than on the trading floor. Learn that the less diversified your portfolio, the more risk there is in your portfolio. Know that regardless of how successful you are in the stock market, the market has a very bad habit of knocking you down when you least expect it. Learn to hope for the best, but plan for the worst—always!

How to Be Diversified

Of course, to be properly diversified, you must first understand what it means to be diversified. Owning *three different types* of REITs is *not* diversification.

Assuming you read the definition of diversification, your objective is to not own too many stocks that belong to the same group. You remember, of course, our beloved wildebeest. In this case, think of the herd as an entire sector of stocks, where each Wildebeest is a different stock. Now, let's assume the herd is merrily romping across the savanna when a pride of lions lunges out of the tall grass right in the path of the herd. In a heartbeat, the whole herd suddenly changes from romping to running hard and moves quickly in the opposite direction. If all your stocks were in that herd, you could go from gaining share price to suddenly losing share price and in a big way.

Diversification

A portfolio strategy designed to reduce exposure to risk by not putting too much of the portfolio's value in any one type or group of stocks, which could all move negatively in the same direction. The ultimate goal of diversification is to reduce or mitigate risk of loss in a portfolio. Risk becomes mitigated by the fact that not all stocks will move up and down in value at the same time or at the same rate. Diversification reduces both the upside and downside potential and allows for more consistent profits over a wide range of markets.

Staying with that analogy, you can think of *industries* as *small* herds of stocks. *Sectors* are *large* herds of stocks. In either case, you do not want to have all of your stocks in a single herd. A good approach to diversification would be to keep a reasonable limit of stocks in each different industry and different sector. That way, you could be reasonably assured that the lions would not attack all herds at the same time from the same direction. In this way, you have lessened your risk to significant loss.

Moving away from the wildebeest analogy, diversification is nothing more than making sure you don't have too much of your money tied up in too few sectors and industries. Since every stock belongs to an industry and a sector, the simplest way to maintain reasonable diversification is to control the percentage of your portfolio by sector and industry.

Currently, there are about 11 sectors and over 250 industries. Every stock belongs to *one and only one* sector and *one and only one* industry. Every industry belongs to *one and only one* sector. Some sectors have dozens of industries and several hundred stocks. Some sectors have only a couple industries and very few stocks. Some industries have many stocks and some have only a few.

INDUSTRY

A category of business activity that describes a very precise business activity (e.g., semiconductors or shipping). This categorization of stocks is based on each company's major source of revenue, competitors, products, markets served, and so on. Every stock belongs to only one industry designation. Every industry belongs to only one sector designation.

SECTOR

A group of similar industries. A sector can be a group of one or several industries. An industry is a group of one or several stocks.

It is not important that you know how many stocks are in each sector and industry as much as you know that sectors are comprised of groups of industries and industries are comprised of groups of stocks.

In this way, you can quantify how much of your portfolio is devoted, by percentage, to sectors and industries.

Following is a series of lists[1] of the 11 major sectors. Below each sector is a list of industries associated with or belonging to the sector.

I show you this list to make sure you understand the granularity of the groupings. Too many times, you hear a comment from a financial pundit stating something about the Energy sector or the Oil sector or the Precious Metals sector. None of those terms are correct. There is no such designation as "Energy sector." There is a "Basic Materials" sector that has a lot of energy-related stocks in various industries, such as Oil and Gas operations, but nowhere is there a designation of "Energy." All this means that various organizations arbitrarily assign a different classification to various groups of stocks. It doesn't matter which nomenclature you use as long as you use the classification to help you stay diversified in your portfolio.

As for this list of sectors and industries, I am totally agnostic. It matters not a bit to me which of these sectors or industries or the stocks contained therein that I select for my portfolios, and I strongly suggest you remain just as agnostic. What matters is whether the stock selected meets your requirements for quality, as defined in all of these Trading Rules and does NOT violate the Diversification Rule.

Following this list, you will learn how to set the limits of how much of your portfolio can be allocated to sectors and industries.

The Basic Materials sector is a group of industries that are involved with the discovery, development, and processing of raw materials. The industries in the Basic Materials sector are:

Industries in the Basic Materials Sector

- Agricultural Chemicals
- Aluminum
- Chemical Manufacturing
- Chemicals—Major Diversified
- Chemicals—Plastics and Rubber

---

1 The sector and industry naming convention is the standard designation provided by Interactive Data Corporation.

- Coal
- Copper
- Gold and Silver
- Gold Industry
- Independent Oil and Gas
- Industrial Metals and Minerals
- Iron and Steel
- Major Integrated Oil and Gas
- Metal Mining
- Miscellaneous Fabricated Products
- Nonmetallic Mineral Mining
- Oil and Gas—Integrated
- Oil and Gas Drilling and Exploration
- Oil and Gas Equipment and Services
- Oil and Gas Operations
- Oil and Gas Pipelines
- Oil and Gas Refining and Marketing
- Oil Well Services and Equipment
- Paper and Paper Products
- Silver
- Specialty Chemicals
- Synthetics

The <u>Capital Goods</u> sector is a relatively small group of industries that are related to the manufacture or distribution of goods. There is a small number of industries, but those industries contain a diverse set of companies. The industries in the Capital Goods sector are:

Industries in the Capital Goods Sector
- Aerospace and Defense
- Construction—Supplies and Fixtures
- Construction Services
- Miscellaneous Capital Goods

The <u>Consumer Cyclical</u> sector is a group of consumer-related industries that are sensitive to business cycles, whose performance is strongly tied to the overall economy. Consumer Cyclical companies tend to make products or provide services that are in lower demand during economic downturns and higher demand during economic upswings. Industries in the Consumer Cyclical sector are:

Industries in the Consumer Cyclical Sector
- Apparel—Accessories
- Audio and Video Equipment
- Auto and Truck Manufacturers
- Auto and Truck Parts
- Furniture and Fixtures
- Jewelry and Silverware
- Photography
- Recreational Products

The <u>Consumer Goods</u> sector includes a wide range of industries' products, from clothing and footwear to household and personal products. Within this diverse sector are the following industries:

Industries in the Consumer Goods Sector
- Appliances
- Auto Manufacturers—Major
- Auto Parts
- Beverages—Brewers
- Beverages—Soft Drinks
- Beverages—Wineries and Distillers
- Business Equipment
- Cigarettes
- Cleaning Products
- Confectioners
- Dairy Products

- Electronic Equipment
- Farm Products
- Food—Major Diversified
- Home Furnishings and Fixtures
- Housewares and Accessories
- Meat Products
- Office Supplies
- Packaging and Containers
- Personal Products
- Photographic Equipment and Supplies
- Processed and Packaged Goods
- Recreational Goods, Other
- Recreational Vehicles
- Rubber and Plastics
- Sporting Goods
- Textile—Apparel Clothing
- Textile—Apparel Footwear and Accessories
- Tobacco Products, Other
- Toys and Games
- Trucks and Other Vehicles

The Consumer Non-Cyclical sector is a group of consumer-related industries that are not sensitive to business cycles, whose performance is not strongly tied to the overall economy. Consumer Non-Cyclical companies tend to make products or provide services that are consistently in demand during all economic fluctuations. Industries in the Consumer Non-Cyclical sector are:

Industries in the Consumer Non-Cyclical sector

- Beverages (Alcoholic)
- Beverages (Nonalcoholic)
- Crops
- Food Processing
- Personal and Household Products

The <u>Financial</u> sector is a group of industries that comprise financial institutions and financial markets. It has often been said that the Financial sector leads the economy into and out of recessions. Industries are included in the Financial sector are:

Industries in the Financial Sector

- Asset Management
- Closed-End Fund—Debt
- Closed-End Fund—Equity
- Closed-End Fund—Foreign
- Consumer Financial Services
- Credit Services
- Diversified Investments
- Foreign Money Center Banks
- Foreign Regional Banks
- Insurance (Accident and Health)
- Insurance (Life)
- Insurance (Property and Casualty)
- Insurance Brokers
- Investment Brokerage—National
- Investment Brokerage—Regional
- Investment Services
- Life Insurance
- Miscellaneous Financial Services
- Money Center Banks
- Mortgage Investment
- Property Management
- Real Estate Development
- Regional—Mid-Atlantic Banks
- Regional—Midwest Banks
- Regional—Northeast Banks
- Regional—Pacific Banks
- Regional—Southeast Banks

- Regional—Southwest Banks
- Regional Banks

The <u>Real Estate Investment Trusts</u> are a group of various types of REITs and include:

Industries in the REIT Sector
- REIT—Diversified
- REIT—Healthcare Facilities
- REIT—Hotel-Motel
- REIT—Industrial
- REIT—Office
- REIT—Residential
- REIT—Retail
- S&Ls—Savings Banks
- Surety and Title Insurance

The <u>Health Care</u> sector is comprised of a group of industries that focus on medical and health care goods or services. Stocks in the Health Care sector are frequently considered to be defensive because the products and services are essential. This means that even during economic downturns, people will still require medical aid and medicine to overcome illness. This consistent demand for goods and services makes this sector less sensitive to business cycle fluctuations. The industries in the Health Care sector are:

Industries in the Health Care Sector
- Biotechnology
- Biotechnology and Drugs
- Diagnostic Substances
- Drug Delivery
- Drug Manufacturers—Major
- Drug Manufacturers—Other

- Drug-Related Products
- Drugs—Generic
- Health Care Plans
- Health Care Facilities
- Home Health Care
- Hospitals
- Long-Term Care Facilities
- Medical Appliances and Equipment
- Medical Equipment and Supplies
- Medical Instruments and Supplies
- Medical Laboratories and Research
- Medical Practitioners
- Specialized Health Services

The Industrial Goods sector is comprised of a group of industries that focus on machinery, manufacturing plants, materials, and other goods or component parts for use or consumption by other industries or firms. Generally, when demand for Consumer Goods increases, the demand for Industrial Goods also increases. The industries in the Industrial Goods sector are:

Industries in the Industrial Goods Sector

- Aerospace-Defense—Major Diversified
- Aerospace-Defense—Products and Services
- Cement
- Diversified Machinery
- Farm and Construction Machinery
- General Building Materials
- General Contractors
- Heavy Construction
- Industrial Electrical Equipment
- Industrial Equipment and Components
- Lumber, Wood Production
- Machine Tools and Accessories

- Manufactured Housing
- Metal Fabrication
- Pollution and Treatment Controls
- Residential Construction
- Small Tools and Accessories
- Textile Industrial
- Waste Management

The <u>Services</u> sector is a group of industries that provide intangible products (services) that are not goods (tangible products) to consumers. Industries included in the Services sector are:

Industries in the Services Sector
- Advertising
- Advertising Agencies
- Air Delivery and Freight Services
- Air Services, Other
- Apparel Stores
- Auto Dealerships
- Auto Parts Stores
- Auto Parts Wholesale
- Basic Materials Wholesale
- Broadcasting—Radio
- Broadcasting—TV
- Broadcasting and Cable TV
- Building Materials Wholesale
- Business Services
- Casinos and Gaming
- Catalog and Mail Order Houses
- CATV Systems
- Communications Services
- Computers Wholesale
- Consumer Services
- Department Stores

- Discount, Variety Stores
- Drug Stores
- Drugs Wholesale
- Education and Training Services
- Electronics Stores
- Electronics Wholesale
- Entertainment—Diversified
- Food Wholesale
- Gaming Activities
- General Entertainment
- Grocery Stores
- Home Furnishing Stores
- Home Improvement Stores
- Hotels and Motels
- Industrial Equipment Wholesale
- Jewelry Stores
- Lodging
- Major Airlines
- Management Services
- Marketing Services
- Medical Equipment Wholesale
- Movie Production, Theaters
- Music and Video Stores
- Personal Services
- Printing and Publishing
- Publishing—Books
- Publishing—Newspapers
- Publishing—Periodicals
- Railroads
- Real Estate Operations
- Recreational Activities
- Regional Airlines
- Rental and Leasing Services
- Research Services

- Resorts and Casinos
- Restaurants
- Retail—Apparel
- Retail—Catalog and Mail Order
- Retail—Department and Discount
- Retail—Home Improvement
- Retail—Specialty
- Retail—Technology
- Schools
- Security and Protection Services
- Shipping
- Specialty Eateries
- Specialty Retail, Other
- Sporting Activities
- Sporting Goods Stores
- Staffing and Outsourcing Services
- Technical Services
- Toy and Hobby Stores
- Trucking
- Wholesale, Other

The Technology sector is a comprised of a group of industries that focus on the application of information in the design, production, and utilization of goods and services, and in the organization of human activities. Industries belonging in the Technology sector are:

Industries in the Technology Sector
- Application Software
- Business Software and Services
- Communication Equipment
- Computer-Based Systems
- Computer Hardware
- Computer Networks
- Computer Peripherals

- Computer Services
- Computer Storage Devices
- Data Storage Devices
- Diversified Communication Services
- Diversified Computer Systems
- Diversified Electronics
- Electronic Instruments and Controls
- Healthcare Information Services
- Information and Delivery Services
- Information Technology Services
- Internet Information Providers
- Internet Service Providers
- Internet Software and Services
- Long Distance Carriers
- Multimedia and Graphics Software
- Networking and Communication Devices
- Personal Computers
- Printed Circuit Boards
- Processing Systems and Products
- Scientific and Technical Instruments
- Security Software and Services
- Semiconductor—Broad Line
- Semiconductor—Integrated Circuits
- Semiconductor—Specialized
- Semiconductor Equipment and Materials
- Semiconductor—Memory Chips
- Semiconductors
- Software and Programming
- Technical and System Software
- Telecom Services—Domestic
- Telecom Services—Foreign
- Wireless Communications

The <u>Transportation</u> sector is comprised of a group of industries that focus on transporting people and/or goods from one physical location to another.

Industries in the Transportation Sector
- Miscellaneous Transportation
- Water Transportation

The <u>Utilities</u> sector is comprised of a group of industries that focus on utilities such as gas and power. The Utilities sector typically performs best when interest rates are falling or remain low. The industries included in the Utilities sector are:

Industries in the Utilities Sector
- Diversified Utilities
- Electric Utilities
- Foreign Utilities
- Gas Utilities
- Natural Gas Utilities
- Water Utilities

A little later in this rule, you will see an example portfolio that is well diversified by sector and industry. Remember, from an agnostic point of view—the view I want you to have—it doesn't matter which stock or which industry or which sector. The right stock within the right industry and the right sector will be determined through your application of Rules in this book, including the Market-Directional Methodology chapter which tells you how to know whether to be bullish, bearish or neutral in your overall investment bias. Once you have selected the stocks you are considering buying, you will use this Diversification Rule and the next rule on Asset Allocation to see if you have sufficient room, on a percentage basis, to add those stocks to your portfolio.

If you already have too much of your portfolio invested in a certain sector or industry, you will have to bypass adding another stock in that sector or industry to your portfolio, *regardless* of how much you want to buy the stock and *regardless* of how great the stock looks from your application of these Rules in your analysis of the stock.

So just how do you determine if you can add a great stock to your portfolio? The answer is all about how you enforce diversification in your portfolio.

How to Enforce Diversification

The wonderful part about following the diversification rule is that it allows you to add further distance between your investment decisions and your emotions. As I have said before, emotions are an anathema to your ability to make money in the stock market.

As I alluded to in my story on failing to heed a strong diversification strategy at the beginning of this rule, markets tend to move up or down in large groups of stocks. At any given time, one sector or industry can be universally surging higher, while another sector or industry is plummeting to decade lows.

When a sector is booming higher, you could buy almost anything in that sector and see great unrealized gains come your way. And, when this happens, there are often dozens of stocks from which to choose. It would be easy to load your portfolio up with stocks from a booming sector that would make you a lot of money, but no sector moves higher indefinitely; and when a sector or industry suddenly falls out of favor, virtually every stock within that industry or sector will tumble lower—some will fall harder, much harder, than others. Odds are, you will get caught in a big pullback in these stocks as the big institutions unload them in order to capture profits. When that time comes—and come it will—you will have a difficult job of getting out of those stocks fast enough. And, if they occupy too large of a position in your portfolio, you could easily lose a significant portion of your net worth.

So it is important to have some kind of control or limit on how many stocks of a certain type you can or should have in your portfolio at any one time, regardless of how strong those stocks might be with regard to share price appreciation.

Like everything else in this book, I have a formula for diversification that should be followed with discipline, and this rule is no exception.

The Diversification Rule: Do not invest more than 30% of the total *value* of your portfolio in any one sector and no more than 20% of the total *value* of your portfolio in any one industry.

As simple as this rule is, it is profoundly helpful as you build, manage, and grow your portfolio of stocks. Often, you will find several great stocks you want to have in your portfolio, and if you were not following this rule, you could easily find yourself significantly over-weighted in one sector or industry.

Staying diversified will help keep you out of trouble. It will help keep you from letting greed manage your portfolio instead of commonsense rules.

Let's go through some examples of what I am talking about. When you decide to add a stock to your portfolio, you need to make several decisions:

1. Is the market in a bullish bias (see Chapter 1, The Market Directional Rule)?
2. Is the stock's Sector in a bullish trend (see Chapter 4, The Technicals Rule)?
3. Is the stock's Industry in a bullish trend (see Chapter 4)?
4. Is the stock in a strong technical trend and above its Transition Zone (see Chapter 4)?
5. Does the stock have a strong fundamental score (see Chapter 2, The Fundamentals Rule)?
6. What percentage of your total portfolio, in terms of NAV (net asset value), is devoted to the stock's Sector (see this Chapter, The Asset Allocation Rule)?

7. What percentage of your total portfolio, in terms of NAV (net asset value), is devoted to the Stock's Industry (see this Chapter, The Asset Allocation Rule)?

8. What percentage of your total portfolio do you plan to invest in this particular stock (see Asset Allocation Rule).

9. If you know you cannot have more than 30% in any one Sector, based on the result of 6, above, how much (on a percentage basis) do you have left to invest in any stock associated with this stock's Sector?

10. If you know you cannot have more than 20% in any one Industry, based on the result of 7, above, how much (on a percentage basis) do you have left to invest in any stock associated with this stock's Industry?

If the answer to number 8 is less than or equal to the answer to number 6; and if the answer to number 8 is less than or equal to the answer to 7; and if the stock meets all the criteria for number 1, number 2, number 3, number 4 and number 5, then buying this stock will not violate your diversification rules.

How to Stay Diversified

Over time, some of the holdings in your portfolio will increase in NAV (Net Asset Value) more than others. It is likely that perhaps some of your holdings will increase in value dramatically. You may have been nicely diversified, according to the 30/20 rule (no more than 30% in any one Sector and no more than 20% in any one Industry) when you initially purchased a holding, but because that holding has significantly increased in share price, it now occupies a larger percentage of your entire portfolio.

Likewise, this would mean that the Sector distribution and the Industry distribution may have changed due to the increased value of one or more holdings.

It is a good idea that, at least once a quarter, you recalculate the percentage allocation your portfolio has for each Industry and each Sector.

If you find that your portfolio has become over-loaded in a Sector or Industry, you should sell enough shares of the holdings that have increased significantly in share price to bring the portfolio back in line with the 30/20 rule.

You will learn in the Asset Allocation Rule that you also need to maintain a reasonably equal allocation of capital across all holdings in your portfolio, so as to not get over-weighted in one position over another. This Rule will assist you in maintaining a diversification strategy that will help mitigate downside risk when one Sector or Industry or stock suddenly reverses trend.

WHAT YOU LEARNED IN THIS RULE

This is a portfolio management rule that shows you how to keep your portfolio properly diversified. In this rule, you learned:

- Why diversification is important and what can happen if your portfolio is not well diversified.
- How to evaluate your portfolio to see how it is currently diversified by calculating the amount of the portfolio that is devoted to each sector and each industry.
- The maximum amount of your portfolio that should be concentrated in any one sector and any one industry.
- To consider both the basis you have in your portfolio by sector and industry, but more importantly, consider the current value of your holdings by sector and industry.
- How to get your current portfolio into proper diversification by selling shares in over-weighted industries and sectors.

CHAPTER 10

THE ASSET ALLOCATION RULE

"The market loves teaching expensive lessons to overconfident investors."

TOTAL INVESTABLE DOLLARS / MAXIMUM NUMBER OF POSITIONS IN PORTFOLIO = PERFECT BALANCE

This Rule is a companion rule to the Diversification Rule. Where the Diversification Rule covered how to keep your portfolio diversified from a Sector and Industry perspective, this Rule covers a problem many investors have, which is how many stocks to own at any one time and how much money should be invested in each position.

This Rule is an amazingly simple rule, but it is extremely important for portfolio management. As a reminder, your objective is to build a world-class portfolio of stocks that will make consistent and significant profits in the stock market.

But making consistent profits in the stock market is more than just picking the right stock at the right time and/or selling the right stock at the right time. It also is about minimizing risk.

How Can I Minimize Risk While Making Profits?

Risk can be defined in many ways, but one element of risk which can and must be avoided is overweighting your stock investments by either having too few positions or putting more money into one position than you put into another.

You see, regardless of how adamant you are with your rules or how closely you stick to my Rules, the market will, on occasion, completely move against you and your best picks. There is no way to avoid this. It will happen just as sure as you are reading this book. One of these days, your best stock pick will turn out to be a real loser. It will completely defy all your rules and all your logic. It will move precipitously against you when you least expect it. Count on it. This will happen to you sooner or later. It happens to every stock market investor.

So, the best way to avoid this reversal of fortune is to never have too much of your net worth tied up in any one position. That way, even if that stock suddenly goes to zero, your total portfolio will not be significantly damaged.

This rule will give you the method and the formula for picking the right size portfolio, in terms of capital and number of positions to have in your portfolio, and it will give you the methodology for keeping your portfolio properly allocated with your investment dollars.

The Diversification Rule and the Asset Allocation Rule are closely related. They are easy concepts and once implemented they function more like an insurance policy for your portfolio than anything else. Everyone understands the need for insurance: homeowners insurance, health, car, life, and so on. Why do you have insurance? It is to cover the cost of an event that could significantly impact your financial stability or the financial stability of others whom you want to protect. There are many reasons to have insurance, but all those reasons boil down to one desire or outcome: to provide enough cash to offset a major loss.

The Diversification Rule and the Asset Allocation rule will mitigate your losses when the market moves against you.

But, here's an important fact. You can follow the Diversification Rule to the letter and still have your portfolio out of balance and, as a consequence, holding far too much risk.

You see, the Diversification Rule takes care of balancing your portfolio from a diversification perspective, but this Rule takes care of balancing your portfolio from an asset allocation perspective. If you recall, I explained in the Diversification Rule how to avoid putting too many eggs in one basket by not letting your portfolio become over-weighted in any one industry or sector.

But, just as important as the Diversification Rule is for diversification, the Asset Allocation Rule keeps you from having too much of your net worth tied up in any single stock. Always assume one of your stocks can go to zero before the market opens tomorrow. What would you do if your largest holding were to suddenly declare bankruptcy overnight and your stock's share price were to drop from $100 to $0 before the market opens the next morning? You haven't even had your first cup of coffee or turned on *Squawk Box* on CNBC! Impossible? Not really. It happens with enough regularity that you should be somewhat paranoid about this Rule. It happened to Bear Stearns in less than 24 hours. Enron took longer, but it still left thousands of investors with $0 in value.

It is important—critically important—to do all you can to mitigate the risk of one of your stock holdings suddenly and catastrophically dropping in price. This kind of event can and will happen to you at some point in your investment life. It will happen when you least expect it. And it will hurt!

Therefore, you must always assume there is the possibility that any stock in your portfolio can suddenly and without warning plummet in price. This is why we use stop losses (see Chapter 5, The Stop Loss Rule). But stop loss orders will do you no good if a stock's price drops from $100 to nearly $0. No one will be buying your stock and a stop loss order will be worthless. This is why we practice industry and sector diversification (see Chapter 9, The Diversification Rule).

And this is why you must also implement Rule 10, The Asset Allocation Rule.

KEEP YOUR PORTFOLIO EQUALLY WEIGHTED

Keeping your portfolio equally weighted means that if you have 20 positions in your portfolio you should have no more than 5% of the *value* of your portfolio in each position. If you have 10 positions, you should have no more than 10% in each position. If you have 50 positions in your portfolio, you should have no more than 2% in each position.

The calculation is extremely simple: Decide how many stocks you are going to have in your portfolio and then divide that number into 100. For a 50-position portfolio, you divide 100 by 50, which is 2. This means no more than 2% of your portfolio should be held by any one position.

So, the next big question should be: How many stocks should you have in your portfolio? Following are some guidelines that will help you make that determination.

- **The amount of cash you plan to invest in the market matters.** The amount of money you plan to put to work in the market may constrain the number of positions you can have in your portfolio. This number is different for every investor. Determining this number can be nontrivial and should include an analysis of your financial condition and objectives.

As a general rule, however, if you have less than $5,000 to invest in the market, you would be wise to just select a broad index fund or an exchange-traded fund (ETF), and not do a lot of trading. If you have less than $5,000 to put into the market, you should not be trying to build a portfolio of stocks.

The primary reason is that in order for you to have a 20-position portfolio, for example, you could not invest more than $250 in each position. Some stocks cost more than $250 per share. But that's not the main reason. The main reason is every time you buy or sell a stock, your broker is going to charge you a transaction fee. Let's assume that fee is only $5. That means every time you make a trade it is costing you 0.1%. It becomes very expensive if you are making several trades a month. Assume you make just 10 trades a month. That amounts to 1% per month in broker fees. Multiply that by 12 and those trades are costing you 12% per year. This means you have to make more than 12% per year just to break even. That is just too high of a hurdle for you to overcome.

In a $10,000 portfolio, it is very difficult to achieve significant annual gains if you make very many trades in a year. In the above example, a $10,000 portfolio will spend 6% per year in trading fees. A $20,000 portfolio is getting far more reasonable. At $20,000, the above scenario results in only a 3% annual cost rate for trading fees. At $40,000, that 3% is down to only 1.5%; and so on.

The more money you can assign to your portfolio for stock trades, the lower your net cost of trades will be and the smaller that cost will be with regard to your net total return.

- **Determine your time management.** Next, you need to think about the amount of time you have available for the research, charting, and formula calculations. Maybe you have lots of time available for this effort. Maybe you have a day job. Maybe you have very limited time. If you follow my Rules for consistent profits in the stock market, you will need at least one hour per week *per position* in your portfolio.
- **Have enough stocks to be properly diversified.** As a general rule of thumb, it is very difficult to be adequately diversified with fewer than 10 positions in your portfolio. However, a 20-position or 30-position portfolio can maintain excellent levels of diversification, especially if you include a few ETFs.

ETF

Similar to an index mutual fund, exchange-traded funds (ETFs) are designed to track different indexes, such as the Russell 2000 Index or the S&P 500 Index, or a particular industrial sector such as utility or biotechnology stocks. ETFs are different than index funds and sector funds because they are legally structured as stocks and are traded on stock exchanges just like any other stock and can be traded intraday and also sold short.

This Rule is all about allocating funds in your portfolio. *Keeping an even distribution is the key element mastering this rule.* To accomplish this task:

CURRENT VALUE OF THE PORTFOLIO

Determined by multiplying the number of shares by the current price of those shares by position held.

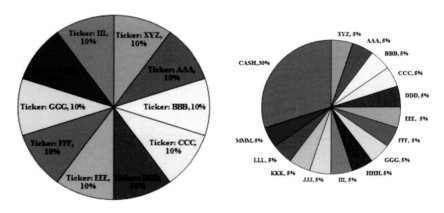

Figure 9.1—Portfolio Asset Allocation by Stock (100% Invested)

Figure 9.2   Portfolio Asset Allocation by Stock (70% Invested)

Figures 9.1 and 9.2 illustrate this concept a bit more graphically. Figure 9.1 represents a perfect value distribution of a 10-position portfolio, assuming it is 100% invested.

Figure 9.2 represents a perfect value distribution of a 20-position portfolio with 30% of the portfolio in cash:

Decide on the total amount of money (cash plus total value of any stocks you own) you are going to devote to your stock portfolio. As your portfolio grows in value, use the net total value of your portfolio for your distribution calculation.

1. Pick the exact number of positions you plan to have in your portfolio assuming you have 100% of your cash invested.
2. Divide the total value of your portfolio (cash plus value of equities) by the total number of positions you will have in your portfolio *when fully invested*. The result of this calculation is the maximum amount of cash you should devote to any one position. If you hold a position that is significantly higher than this amount, you might consider selling enough shares to bring it into compliance.
3. Keep your positions exactly at an even distribution. This does not mean you should be continually buying a few shares or selling a few shares just for the sake of balancing. Remember, each trade costs you a trading fee and you want to keep those fees to a minimum. Therefore, a good rule of thumb is to make adjustments only when a position gets more than 30% over its ideal distribution level. For example: Assume you have a 10-position portfolio and you bought a stock using 10% of the value of your portfolio. A little later down the road, that stock moves higher in price to where it is now occupying 13% of your total portfolio (that would be a 30% profit in that one position). At that time, you should consider selling enough shares to bring the total value of the position back to 10% of your total portfolio, remembering, of course, that your portfolio has grown in total value.

This math may seem a bit obtuse, but if you list your portfolio tickers, the number of shares, the basis for each position, and the current price, you can use a simple Excel worksheet to calculate the totals and percentages, making this process relatively easy.

WHAT YOU LEARNED IN THIS RULE

Remember, balancing your risk pays off in the long run, like a good insurance policy. Since there is no real insurance policy available for investing in the stock market (aside from using options, which are not covered in this book), we are obligated to implement one for ourselves, by keeping your investment risks to a minimum.

In this rule, you learned:

- That diversification by industry and sector is not enough insurance against a catastrophic corporate failure.
- To never invest more money in one stock than you do in another. This doesn't have to be exact, but it should be within a 10th of a percent one way or the other from an equal distribution amount.
- To readjust the asset allocation in your portfolio when one of your holdings gets disproportionately over-weighted due to increasing share price.

MAKING THE COMMITMENT TO BEING A RULES-BASED INVESTOR

Thank you for spending a few hours with me. I hope you enjoyed reading and studying my market-directional rules-based approach to investing in the stock market. I hope you have become more empowered to take control of your investments. I know from personal experience that your use of these rules will make you a wealthier, happier, and less stressed stock market investor.

Let's agree on one simple objective: You want to make consistent profits in the stock market.

I believe I have given you the rules and methodology to make that happen. This book was written with that objective in mind. I want this to now become your objective; notice I didn't say it is your "goal."

GOAL
- The purpose towards which an endeavor is directed
- Not strictly measurable or tangible
- Generic in action

OBJECTIVE
- Something that one's efforts or actions are intended to accomplish
- Measurable and tangible
- Has specific actions in order to achieve

Goals are great, but they often have the connotation of being just beyond our capabilities. Objectives, however, are definitely achievable.

For any objective worth achieving, there has to be a plan and a willingness to perform the necessary steps to attain the objective. My plan is for you to agree to follow my rules and methodology by making the commitment to a disciplined course of action. Discipline is the absolute key to your success in this plan. You cannot follow some of the rules and part of the methodology, and expect to be consistently profitable. You cannot follow these rules some of the time, and be consistently profitable.

You have to commit to following all the rules and the entire methodology all of the time—in good markets, bad markets, and trading-range markets. Does it take work? Yes. Will it be worth it? Absolutely!

You must be committed to letting these rules govern the way you buy and sell stocks. You must be committed to replacing emotion with these rules. Don't get me wrong; there will be plenty of opportunities for you to have an opinion based on current events, but not to the extent that your opinion violates these rules. While you are perfectly capable of creating your own, personalized set of rules, the rules in this book are tried and tested. They work and will work for you if, and only if, you have the consistent discipline to follow them.

I want you to be a consistent winner in your stock investments. This, by the way, does *not* mean that every trade will make you a profit. Making consistent profits means that, over time, you will make a greater number of profitable trades than losing trades. Your losing trades will have consistently smaller losses, while your winning trades will have consistently larger gains.

Remember, the key here is discipline. Don't give up and don't give in to your emotions. These rules work. They always work. You can absolutely bank on it.

Make these rules a part of your investment DNA and you will do well. Put them to work. You won't regret it!

Now, get out there and start making some serious money!

UNDERSTANDING
STOP LOSS ORDERS

First, let's make sure you clearly understand just what a stop loss order is and what it is not:

There are three kinds of stop loss orders:

1. **Stop limit.** This is an order that says once the stock's market price touches or goes below the stop limit order price, the stop limit order is activated, but not necessarily filled. The broker is required to sell the stock at or above the stop limit order price, if, and only if, there is a willing buyer who will pay the limit order price. Should the market price of the stock fall well below the stop limit order price (this is considered a "gap down"), then, although your stop limit order has been activated, it will not fill unless the market price of your stock rebounds back to or above your limit order price. Once the market price of your stock has plummeted below your stop limit order price, it could continue to move lower (even to zero) and your stop limit order will never fill. I do recommend using stop limit orders, but it is important to understand there will be times when you will

have to make a decision about selling a position at a price lower than the stop limit order price.

2. **Stop market.** This type of stop loss order is known by various names, such as "stop," "stop loss," and "stop market." This is an order that says once the stock's market price touches or goes below the stop market order price, the stop market order is activated and filled as soon as there is a willing buyer (market), regardless of price. On the surface, this may sound very disconcerting. It is quite the contrary. If a stock is going to trigger your stop loss price, even if it gaps below your stop loss price, you will want to <u>get out of the stock as quickly as possible.</u>

I believe in the cockroach theory. The theory is there is never only one cockroach. In the case of stocks, if a stock plummets below your stop loss setting, it is almost always a result of some kind of bad news (the cockroach). And, almost always, not all bad news comes out at once. More bad news (more cockroaches) is likely to follow. *Better to get out at any price than to hope the bad news will go away and the stock will rebound.* Hope is a terrible investment strategy.

3. **Trailing stop.** Trailing stops are designed to follow the market price of a stock by a percentage amount or a fixed dollar amount. The higher the market price of the stock, the higher the trailing stop. If the stock's market price moves lower, the trailing stop *will not* move.

The concept involves just setting the maximum amount that a stock can move lower to trigger the stop. Once the market price of the stock touches or goes below the trailing stop price, the stock is then sold at market to the next willing buyer. **<u>I rarely use trailing stops unless my goal is to sell a holding that could be temporarily trending higher.</u>** Trailing stops are virtually guaranteed to take you out of a position. Each little uptick in a stock's price will pull the stop loss order higher and higher, eventually triggering the stop on the next downtick of the stock's market price.

Here is an example of why I don't like trailing stops:

Let's say that you own a stock that was trading at $40 per share when the market opened on Monday and you had a $4 trailing stop. At the following Friday close, the stock was trading at $60 per share.

Of course, you would expect your stop not to have triggered and that now it is sitting at $56.

What you don't know is that you stopped out at $38 per share. Here is how it happened:

- The stock moved to $42 per share. When it did, the trailing stop moved to $38 per share.
- Then, the stock moved to $38 per share and you stopped out.
- Then, the stock moved back up to $40, then $45, then $50, and finally $60 per share.

If you had used a stop market of $36 per share, your stop would not have triggered, because the stock never traded at or below $36.

It is important that you give a stock enough room for normal volatility. Placing your stops too close to the market price (i.e. well within the expected move) is just asking for a stop out. This is why I generally adjust my stops only once a week.

Regardless of the type of stop loss order, you are *not* guaranteed that you will get your price. All a stop loss order does is provide a "trigger price," such that when the market price of a stock touches or goes below that trigger price, a trade is activated, but not necessarily filled.

APPENDIX B

SCORING THE FUNDAMENTALS

W hen it comes to deciding which stocks to buy, you have learned that 50% of your decision must be based on the stock's fundamentals. In Chapter 2, The Fundamentals Rule, you learned that there are a few fundamentals that matter more than others when selecting stocks. These are called Demand Fundamentals, and are listed below:

- Quarter-over-quarter revenue growth rate
- Quarter-over-quarter earnings growth rate
- Year-over-year revenue growth rate
- Year-over-year earnings growth rate
- Multi-Year revenue growth rate
- Multi-Year earnings growth rate
- Relative PE Ranking
- Return on Equity
- Dividend Yield
- Institutional Holding
- Stock Price
- Relative Fundamental Ranking

Investors tend to have a significant reaction to changes in these fundamentals. The better the numbers, the more investors will drive up demand for shares and, consequently, the higher the price of shares. Therefore, when selecting stocks to buy, the stronger these Demand Fundamentals, the better. Remember, your objective is to own stocks that have the highest likelihood of increasing share price.

In Rule 3, you learned of an additional key fundamental that is based on relative value, where you compare a stock's PE to its peer group or industry.

Certainly, it is a straightforward process to compare all stocks in your universe by these Demand Fundamentals. All you have to do is calculate the rates of growth (or find one of the many free services online that calculate these rates for you) for each stock and compare the results of one stock to another.

The task of finding these Demand Fundamentals is not hard, but it does become a little daunting to have twelve different values for each stock and attempt to find the best stock by comparing these seven values from stock to stock.

I have developed a simple way to quickly find the stock with the best Demand Fundamentals, and it is something you can easily do on your own.

The first thing you will want to do is assign a numeric score to each Demand Fundamental. I score each one from a low of zero to a high of nine. Then, all you have to do is add up the scores for each stock's Demand Fundamentals to get a total score. The stock with the highest score has the best Demand Fundamentals. The stock with the lowest score has the worst.

Below is a suggested scoring template to use for each of the Demand Fundamentals. Following this section is a simple Excel worksheet that shows you how easy it is to rate and rank dozens of stocks with regard to this important fundamental analysis.

SCORING THE FUNDAMENTALS

- **Quarter-over-quarter revenue growth rate:**
  Maximum Score = 15

Scoring quarter-over-quarter revenue growth rates requires that you first calculate the rate of growth from the year-ago quarter results for revenue to the most recent quarter results for revenue. Then, assign a score to these results. To calculate the rate of revenue growth, measure how much a stock's total revenue increased or decreased from the amount of revenue generated by the company in the year-ago quarter to the most recent quarter.

For example, let's assume Company XYZ had quarterly revenue in the year-ago quarter of 10%. In the most recently reported quarter, the company reported revenue of 10.2%. The rate of growth would be $(10.2\% - 10\%)/10\% \times 100 = 2\%$.

Once you have the rate of growth between the year-ago quarter and the most recent quarter, for total revenue, your next step is to assign a score for the results. The following is a recommended scoring structure for this Demand Fundamental:

- 15 for rates greater than or equal to 20%.
- 10 for rates greater than or equal to 10% and less than 20%.
- 7 for rates greater than or equal to 5% and less than 10%.
- 5 for rates greater than or equal to 0% and less than 5%.
- 3 for rates greater than or equal to -5% and less than 0%.
- 0 for rates less than -5%.
- **Quarter-over-quarter earnings growth rate:**
  Maximum Score = 15

Compare the total earnings for the quarter, one year ago, to the total earnings for the most recent quarter, and then determine the percentage increase or decrease. For example, let's assume Company XYZ had quarterly earnings in the year-ago quarter of 5%. In the most recently reported quarter, the company reported earnings of 10%. The rate of growth would be (10% - 5%) ÷ 5% × 100 = 100%. Earnings growth of 100% is huge, and investors will pay up for these shares.

The scoring for this Demand Fundamental is:

- 15 for rates greater than 20%.
- 10 for rates greater than 10% and less than 20%.
- 7 for rates greater than 5% and less than 10%.
- 5 for rates greater than 0% and less than 5%.
- 3 for rates greater than -5% and less than 0%.
- 0 for rates less than -5%.
- **Year-over-year revenue growth rate: Maximum Score = 10**

Compare the total revenue growth rate for the previous year to the total revenue growth rate for the most recent year, and then determine the percentage increase or decrease. For example, let's assume Company XYZ had an annual revenue growth rate last year of 10%. In the most recently reported year, the company reported a revenue growth rate of 9%. The rate of growth would be (9% - 10%) ÷ 10% × 100 = -10%. The revenue growth rate of this company went down by 10%.

The scoring for this Demand Fundamental is:

- 10 for rates greater than 30%.
- 7 for rates greater than 15% and less than 30%.
- 4 for rates greater than 5% and less than 15%.
- 2 for rates greater than 0% and less than 5%.
- 1 for rates greater than -5% and less than 0%.
- 0 for rates less than -5%.
- **Year-over-year earnings growth rate: Maximum Score = 10**

Compare the total earnings growth rate for the previous year to the total earnings growth rate for the most recent year, and then determine the percentage increase or decrease. For example, let's assume Company XYZ had annual earnings growth rate last year of 14%. In the most recently reported year, the company reported earnings of 8%. The rate of growth would be (8% - 14%) ÷ 14% × 100 = -42%. The growth rate of this company went down by 42%!

The scoring for this Demand Fundamental is:

- 10 for rates greater than 30%.
- 7 for rates greater than 15% and less than 30%.
- 4 for rates greater than 5% and less than 15%.
- 2 for rates greater than 0% and less than 5%.
- 1 for rates greater than -5% and less than 0%.
- 0 for rates less than -5%.
- **Multi-Year earnings growth rate. Maximum Score = 8**

Go back six years and calculate the rate of growth of earnings from year 5 to year 4, then from year 4 to year 3, and so on, until you have the yearly earnings growth rate for each year. Then, add these five rates together and divide by five for the five-year average earnings growth rate. For example, let's assume Company XYZ had the following annual earnings growth rates for the previous five years: 2%, 5%, 3%, 8%, and 9%. The average annual earnings growth rate would be (2% + 5% + 3% + 8% + 9%) ÷ 5 = 5.4%.

The scoring for this Demand Fundamental is:

- 8 for rates greater than 50%.
- 6 for rates greater than 25% and less than 50%.
- 4 for rates greater than 5% and less than 25%.
- 2 for rates greater than 0% and less than 5%.
- 1 for rates greater than -5% and less than 0%.
- 0 for rates less than -5%.
- **Multi-year revenue growth rate. Maximum Score = 8**

Go back six years and calculate the rate of growth of revenue from year 5 to year 4, then from year 4 to year 3, and so on, until you have the yearly revenue growth rate for each year. Then add these five rates together and divide by five for the 5-year average revenue growth rate. For example, let's assume Company XYZ had the following annual revenue growth rates for the previous five years: 12%, 5%, 30%, 10% and 12%. The average revenue earnings growth rate would be (12% + 5% + 30% + 10% + 12%) ÷ 5 = 7.8%.

The scoring for this Demand Fundamental is:

- 8 for rates greater than 50%.
- 6 for rates greater than 25% and less than 50%.
- 4 for rates greater than 5% and less than 25%.
- 2 for rates greater than 0% and less than 5%.
- 1 for rates greater than -5% and less than 0%.
- 0 for rates less than -5%.
- **Relative PE Ranking. Maximum Score = 6**

It is always important to pay the least amount for the best stocks. This is another way to say you want to buy the stocks with the most value. Value is measured in terms of earnings and the amount of dollars it takes to buy those earnings. PE is nothing more than the price of a stock divided by its most recent earnings per share. This is a very good way of comparing one stock's value (PE) to another.

But, as you learned in Rule 3, the only time that this comparison should be done is when comparing a stock's PE to another stock in its peer (or industry) group.

You can know how expensive or cheap (from a value perspective) a stock is by comparing its PE to the average PE of its industry. If the stock's PE is much higher than the average PE of its industry, it is considered *overvalued*. If its PE is much lower than the average PE of its industry, it is considered *undervalued*.

The following is a suggested methodology for scoring each stock's Relative PE:

- First, determine the PE for each stock in the stock's industry (i.e. "Peer Group").
- Next, sort the Peer Group by PE with the lowest PE at the top.
- Find where the stock being scored ranks in the list of PEs.
- Finally, divide the position of the stock in the list of the stock's peers by the total number of stocks in the stock's Peer Group.
- Now, score the Relative PE by the following scoring method:

- 6 for a stock in the best 10% of Peer Group PEs
- 5 for a stock in the next best 10% of Peer Group PEs
- 4 for a stock in the next best 25% of Peer Group PEs
- 3 for a stock in the next best 25% of Peer Group PEs
- 2 for a stock in the next best 25% of Peer Group PEs
- 1 for a stock in the worst 5% of Peer Group PEs
- **Return on Equity. Maximum Score = 5**

Return on equity is the return generated by the company for each dollar of shareholder investment. This is a way to determine how effectively the shareholder's investment is being employed by the company. This value needs to be 15% or higher; the higher the better. Return on equity is calculated by dividing the annual earnings by common shareholder equity, which is equal to total assets minus total liabilities.

The scoring for this Demand Fundamental is:

- 5 for rates greater than 15%.
- 4 for rates greater than 12% and less than 15%.
- 3 for rates greater than 10% and less than 12%.
- 2 for rates greater than 5% and less than 12%.
- 1 for rates greater than 0% and less than 5%.
- 0 for rates less than 0%.
- **Dividend Yield. Maximum Score = 5**

Stocks with high-paying dividends are not always the best stocks to own for significant growth in share price. But, in those rare instances where a stock's other Demand Fundamentals are strong *and* that stock happens to have a strong dividend, you can certainly consider that a big plus. Most investors prefer higher-yielding stocks for if a company increases its dividend, it generally gets a nice bump up in share price. Therefore, dividend yield is another one of the Demand Fundamentals, which is scored as the following:

- 5 for yields equal to or greater than 7%.
- 3 for yields greater than 4% and less than 7%.
- 1 for yields greater than 0% and less than 4%.
- 0 for yields less than or equal to 0%.
- **Institutional Ownership. Maximum Score = 6**

One does not normally think of institutional ownership as a fundamental, but for 99% of investors it should be. In fact, it should be considered a fundamental for any investor other than an institutional investor. You learned in Chapter 8, The Institutional Ownership Rule, that we, as individual investors, can make certain assumptions about the strength and quality of a company by the number of outstanding shares owned by institutions.

You learned that if institutions own too many outstanding shares, the risk of a major and rapid sell-off is increased. You also learned that if a company has no institutional ownership, it means the big institutions have reviewed the company's potential to generate increasing share price and passed. In other words, a company with no institutional ownership is considered fundamentally weak.

So, it is a good idea to rate and score institutional ownership as follows:

- 0 for institutional ownership greater than 98%.
- 1 for institutional ownership greater than 95% and less than 98%.
- 4 for institutional ownership greater than 60% but less than 95%.

- 6 for institutional ownership greater than 30% and less than 60%.
- 4 for institutional ownership greater than 4% and less than 30%.
- 1 for institutional ownership greater than 0% and less than 4%.
- 0 for institutional ownership of 0%.
- **Stock Price. Maximum Score = 4**

You may not think that the price of a stock is a fundamental, and in a pure sense, it is not. However, the price of a stock often reflects the perceived value of the company behind the stock. Another way to think about it is this way... A $1 stock is a $1 stock, because it deserves its worth of only $1. While I know this somewhat flies in the face of PE analysis where value is taken into account, there is some limited value in scoring a stock's price just from a market-perceived value perspective.

On the other end of the spectrum are the very high-priced equities. When a stock's share price gets too high, the demand for those shares tends to diminish, just because the rank-and-file investment community cannot afford to buy enough shares to make the risk worthwhile. In other words, a stock's share price can just be too expensive for most investors to own, regardless of how valuable it is. This loss of demand is worth including in your fundamental analysis.

So, it is a good idea to rate and score the share price of a stock as follows:

- 0 for stocks priced over $250 per share.
- 4 for stocks priced over $20 per share and less than $250 per share.
- 1 for stocks priced over $5 per share and less than $20 per share.
- 0 for stocks priced below $5 per share.
- **Relative Fundamental Ranking. Maximum Score = 8**

Much like the process you go through to rate, rank and score the "Relative PE" of a stock, it is a good idea to rate, ransk and score the "Relative Fundamentals" of a stock. In other words, score how each stock's fundamental score stacks up against all the other stocks in that stock's Peer Group.

The first thing to do is collect the total Fundamental Score of each stock in the stock's Peer Group, *excluding* the Relative Fundamental Score of each stock. This means that the maximum score of any stock will be 100 − 8 = 92. Why? Because the maximum score for Relative Fundamentals is 8. So, each stock can only have a maximum of 92 points in Fundamental Score.

Below is how to score Relative Fundamentals:

- First, determine the total Fundamental Score for each stock in the stock's industry (i.e. "Peer Group"). Do NOT include the Relative Fundamental Score of each stock when determining this total Fundamental Score.
- Next, sort the Peer Group by total Fundamental Score, with the highest score at the top
- Find where the stock being scored ranks in the list of Fundamental Scores
- Finally, divide the position of the stock in the list of the stock's peers by the total number of stocks in the stock's Peer Group.
- Now, score the Relative Fundamentals by the following method:
- 8 for a stock in the best 10% of the Peer Group Fundamental Scores
- 6 for a stock in the next best 10% of the Peer Group Fundamental Scores
- 4 for a stock in the next best 25% of the Peer Group Fundamental Scores
- 2 for a stock in the next best 25% of the Peer Group Fundamental Scores

- 1 for a stock in the next best 25% of the Peer Group Fundamental Scores
- 0 for falling into the bottom 5% of the Peer Group Fundamental Scores

APPENDIX C

PROVING THE CONCEPT

What follows are the results of back-testing the Market-Directional Investing Methodology by decade, starting in 1950. The purpose of this 'proof-of-concept' is that I did not cherry-pick on certain date ranges to prove that Market-Directional Investing works. You will see that Market-Directional Investing outperforms buy-and-hold in every decade. In some cases, the methodology produces substantially better results than others, but in 100% of the back-tests in every single time-period from 1950 to 2017, the methodology lowered risk, was always profitable and outperformed the market **EVERY SINGLE TIME**

Starting with the decade of the 50s...(see Figure C-1)

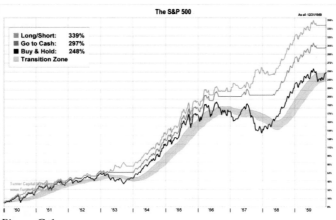

Figure C-1

You should notice that the buy-and-hold crowd (black line, Figure 1) looked pretty good until 1956. That is when the market went into a two-year see-saw bear market correction. Notice the false bull-market spike in mid-1957, followed by a huge sell-off.

My 'Go-to-Cash' mode made 248% over the 10-year period and mostly avoided the big downturns in late 1956 and the second half of 1957.

Using this methodology, you could have taken huge losses off the table, avoided all of that downside risk and still beat the market by 49%. The Go-to-Cash approach is 100% in the market when it is trading above the Transition Zone, and 100% in cash when it is inside or below the Zone.

But, now look at the top line where the model shorted the market when it was trading below the Transition Zone, instead of staying in cash. The long/short approach is 100% in the market when the market is above the Zone, 100% in cash when the market is inside the Zone, and 100% short the market when the market is below the Zone. This results in an improvement over buy-and-hold of more than 91%.

Moving on to the 60s... (see Figure C-2)

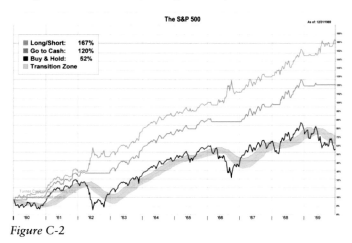

Figure C-2

The decade of the 60s (Figure C-2) was not a good decade for the buy-and-hold crowd. While they did turn a profit of 52% over 10 years, they far underperformed Market-Directional Investing AND buy-and-hold had all that risk of huge losses (see 1962, 1966 and even 1969).

Using the Go-to-Cash component of my Market-Directional approach (the middle line on the chart), it outperformed buy-and-hold by more than 68%!

The top line (Long/Short) was even better. Using the process of being 100% long the market as long as it was trading above the Transition Zone, 100% in cash when the market was inside the Transition Zone, and 100% short when the market was below the Transition Zone, produced a 10-year return of 167%. That is more than 3 times better than buy-and-hold. And, I know I am beating a dead horse here (can you still say that in today's PC world?), this methodology had no (zero) major losses that buy-and-hold experienced in 1962, 1966 and 1969.

Now for the 70s... (see Figure C-3)

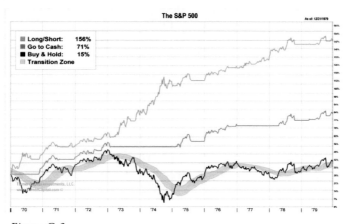

Figure C-3

Don't feel too bad for the buy-and-hold crowd in the decade of the 70s (Figure C-3)...there is a much worse one coming.

The buy-and-hold approach generated a dismal 15% gain after holding on for 10 long years. I'm sure Bogle or Siegel or Buffett do not use this decade to prove the merits of buy-and-hold.

Notice the 2+ year bear market of 1973 through 1974. If you were using my Market-Directional methodology, you would not have suffered through those years with massive losses.

The Go-to-Cash mode of my Market-Directional approach generated a decent 71% over the 10 years (4.7 times better than buy-and-hold), and avoided all the major losses in 1971, 1973, 1974 and 1977.

The Long/Short mode of Market-Directional Investing produced even greater returns. By being 100% in the market when the market was trading above the yellow band ("Transition Zone"), 100% in cash when the market was trading inside the Zone, and 100% short the market when it was trading below the Zone...it produced a staggering 156%. That is more than 10 times (1000%) better than buy-and-hold!

You might be thinking...Market-Directional Investing cannot be this good all the time, can it? Actually, I have never seen it underperform buy-and-hold, except for very short periods of time.

Here come the 80s...(see Figure C-4)

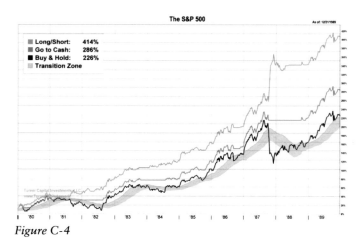

Figure C-4

This (Figure C-4) is an interesting decade. I want you to pay particular attention to the latter half of 1987. Now, that is a serious correction!

Look closely at how the Go-to-Cash model worked. It obviously lost a little when the pull-back started, but it took you out just slightly after the market topped and before the market plunged lower.

Granted, due to all the risk on the table, it did not get you back into the market until late 1988, but long before the buy-and-hold crowd got back to even in 1989.

The decade of the 80s was much better for the buy-and-hold crowd, but far less productive than Market-Directional Investing.

The Go-to-Cash approach of Market-Directional Investing generated 286%, compared to 226% for buy-and-hold. The Long/Short approach of Market-Directional Investing generated a whopping 414%—nearly twice that of buy-and-hold. In both the Go-to-Cash and the Long/Short approaches, neither of them suffered any major loss in the entire decade—even the huge sell-off in 1987 left both of these approaches unscathed.

Next Up? The Decade of the 90s... (see Figure C-5)

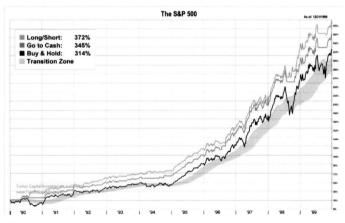

Figure C-5

Finally, a decade where the buy-and-hold crowd can crow about their performance (Figure C-5). Granted, it still underperformed both the Go-to-Cash and the Long/Short approach, but not by a whole lot.

The decade of the 90s was, for the most part (except for 1998 and 1999) a good decade for everyone.

The Go-to-Cash approach beat the buy-and-hold approach by about 31% on a net comparison basis. The Long/Short approach did better: beating buy-and-hold by 58% on a net comparison basis.

But just wait until you see what happens in the first decade of the new century...

The 2000s... (see Figure C-6)

Figure C-6

You might notice that it is hard to find anyone in the buy-and-hold crowd bragging about the first 10 years of this new century. The chart (Figure C-6) explains why.

Buying on the first trading day of 2000 and holding for the following 10 years generated an abysmal return for buy-and-hold... down an atrocious -24%.

While the Go-to-Cash strategy was up a respectable +82%, you should notice that it kept you out of the market from near the top in 2000 until after the bottom in 2003. It did the same for you by getting you out of the market in late 2007, and not back in until after the risk was diminished in 2009. Keep in mind that not one single time did this methodology do any forecasting or guessing. 100% of the time, it gave buy and sell signals AFTER THE FACT. When the market moved from above the Transition Zone to inside the Transition Zone, the signal went from bullish to 'move-to-cash,' and it did not give the buy signal again until the market had moved back up above the Transition Zone.

The Long/Short strategy was even better, up a huge +160%, while the buy-and-hold strategy was down -24%.

Now, the 2010s...or as much as I know at this writing (see Figure C-7)

Figure C-7

As I write this chapter, the second decade of this century (Figure C-7) has not completed. So far, though, as you can see, the Market-Directional approach is far ahead of the buy-and-hold approach.

The bottom-line is this: Market-Directional Investing ALWAYS outperforms buy-and-hold, AND it dramatically reduces risk of loss in bear trending markets. In my opinion, buy-and-hold is one of the riskiest strategies ever devised, primarily perpetuated by people and entities that have a vested interest in making you 'think' it is the best investment strategies you could follow.

ACKNOWLEDGEMENTS

I want to thank several people who have helped me along the way to this exciting world of stock market trading.

First, I want to thank the professors at Oklahoma State University where I obtained my degree in civil engineering. They instilled in me the belief that, with the right set of rules and formulas, there isn't any problem that cannot be solved.

The next person I want to thank is Augie Gale. He would be surprised to find himself mentioned here. If only you had whispered in my ear, "Go into the stock market, Mike," it would have not taken me so long to arrive at this wonderful place. I am grateful he ignited the spark.

To my loyal partners in this business, I want to thank you for your sound counsel. I appreciate your dedication to our purpose of helping individual investors reach their financial dreams. Where would I be today if I hadn't met these wonderful people! Thank you for believing in me. Thank you for your optimism and can-do attitude!

Special thanks to my son, Will, who was instrumental in the design and development of the database and programming algorithms we use every day to analyze thousands of stocks in our database. Your work on creating our tools (both the public and the private versions) has and continues to be phenomenal. Christie (Will's wife), thank you for your help and support for the long hours and, seemingly, never-ending late-night programming.

For our daughter, Amy, thank you for all those years growing up in the company...attending the tradeshows...bypassing the unions to get our booth set up...always trying to squeeze time in every spare moment with laughter, grandchildren events and unflagging support for your mom and me. Bryan (Amy's husband), thank you for your unwavering support.

And to my grandchildren (Alex, Kate, Kailey and Aidan) who have crawled on my lap while I've worked and asked, "What are stocks, Pop?" and, amazingly, still believe I am larger than life. When I couldn't attend a particular family function, or I was late to others, you always understood. I am grateful for your love and affection.

Thank you to all my subscribers, friends and clients who call and email me with encouraging words. I take your thoughts to heart and appreciate them more than you know. Working for you is a joy, and I love every minute of it.

And last, but certainly not least, a special thanks to the love of my life; my wife, Sue, through hours of reading, rereading, and editing, who has never lost her zeal for this work. Thank you for your faith, encouragement, and for allowing me to reach for my dreams. Thank you for being the best partner, friend and supporter in the world! You're the Best, my love.

ABOUT THE AUTHOR

Mike Turner is the founder of TurnerTrends, an online, subscription-based advisory service, which provides his clients with the investor tools for selecting the best equities with the strongest fundamentals and technicals. Many of his subscribers are building and managing their own world-class portfolios using the stock analysis software tools he has developed. His newsletter is gaining in popularity as a result of his unique stock-selling methodology, which he has patented, called the Intelligent Stop Loss®.

Mr. Turner is also the founder, president and Chief Portfolio Manager of Turner Capital Investments, LLC, which is a registered investment advisory. It is through Turner Capital that Mike and his staff manage money for higher net worth clients.

He is a much-sought-after speaker at investment trading venues around the country, including the World MoneyShow, Trader's Expo, and American Association of Individual Investors (AAII) meetings. His advice on stock selection, stock selling, exchange-traded funds (ETFs), and his Market-Directional methodology are his most popular topics.

Mr. Turner graduated from Oklahoma State University with a degree in civil engineering. It is his analytical background, extensive computer skills, and common-sense approach to the stock market that allowed him to develop the powerful software system that analyzes over 6,000 stocks every week. This program sifts through the data to help him find and select good stocks to buy, as well as indicate the time to sell. This information has allowed his clients the opportunity to realize their financial dreams in bull markets and bear markets.

Prior to his involvement in the stock market, Mr. Turner was the founder, developer and president of a company that wrote enterprise-level software systems that were used by medical research facilities and pharmaceutical companies worldwide. His clients included nearly all of the world's major pharmaceutical companies and medical research facilities that were doing preclinical drug safety studies. He was there until he sold his company in 1997.

Mr. Turner is currently the editor of his weekly online newsletter (*Signal Investor* at www.TurnerTrends.com) and serves as the portfolio manager of each of the Turner Capital Investments portfolios (www. TurnerCapitalInvestments.com).

INDEX